KT-446-924

DUNHUANG & SILK ROAD

Compiler: Du Doucheng, Wang Shuqing

Sea Sky Publishing House

(Shenzhen • China)

Duty Editor: *Chen Xingzhun*
Cover Designer: *ZhaoYunshan*
Duty Copy-editor: *WangYing*

责任编辑：陈邢准
封面设计：赵云三
责任技编：王 颖

The picture information in this book comes from Dunhuang Academe

本书图片资料由敦煌研究院提供

DUNHUANG & SILK ROAD

Compiler: *Du Doucheng, Wang Shuqing*
Translator:*Feng Bingyun Gao Changchun ZhongWenqun*
Publisher: *Sea Sky Publishing House*
Address: *Sea Sky Bldg., Caitian Southern Road, Shenzhen P.R.C.*
Post Code: *518033*
Plate making: *Sea Sky Electronic Publishing Co., Ltd.*
Typographer: *Shenzhen Jiaxinda Printing Co.,Ltd*
Format:*889mm × 1194mm 1/24*
Word Count: *80,000*
Printed Order: *1st Edition, May. 2005*
Number: 1-1000

ISBN 7-80697-402-4/G·82
PRICE RMB 98.00

书 名 敦煌与丝绸之路

编 著 杜斗城 王书庆
翻 译 冯秉耘 高长春 钟文群
出版发行者 海天出版社
地 址 深圳市彩田南路海天综合大厦
邮 编 518033
排版制作 海天电子图书开发公司 83460730
印 刷 者 深圳市佳信达印务有限公司
开 本 889mm × 1194mm 1/24
字 数 80千
版 次 2005年5月第1版
印 数 1-1000册

ISBN 7-80697-402-4/G·82
定 价：98.00元

Copyright by Sea Sky Publishing House. All rights reserved.
No part of this publication may be reproduced in any form or by any means without prior written permission of Sea Sky Publishing House. For customer service,
call 86-755-83460234, 86-937-8836349

海天版图书版权所有，侵权必究。
海天版图书凡有印装质量问题，请随时向承印厂调换。
举报电话：(0755)83460234 (0937)8836349

Contents

Dunhuang and Silk-road

Silk-road, known as the "friendship canal" based upon the silk trade between the west and the east, ever extended for thousands of miles (Li) and passed 2000-odd years, is still prosperous now. Silk-road, as it were an old song, a romantic verse as well as an friend ship road, is eternal.Dunhuang holds quite important place in the Chinese and Western history related to the communication and the cultural exchange. Many scholars figuratively use "present-day Shanghai" for Dunhuang in the Han and Tang Dynasties appropriately because of its location of being the general center for the Chinese and Western communication in ancient China. Dunhuang, since the Han, Tang and Song Dynasties, was the northwest region's barrier in both politics and militaries, and also the base for the interior regimes to manage the Western Lands. In the Han Dynasty, four prefectures, playing important roles in both politics and militaries, were set up in Hexi region. Dunhuang prefecture was regarded as the most of all because of its key position in international trade and cultural exchange. In those very days, especially the time of Buddhism being introduced into the central plains from the Western Lands, Dunhuang played the role of being the goods-assembling center and transfer station, thus Dunhuang's weightiness can be seen. Dunhuang was denominated at the time when the emperor Wu of the Han Dynasty set up the prefectures in Hexi region. Ying Shao, a scholar in the Eastern Han Dynasty, annotated the word of Dunghuang, the Dung denoted "big", Huang denoted "prosperity", for reasons given above, Dunghuang is said the prosperous city in the Western Han Dynasty. Li Ji-pu, in the Tang Dynasty, annotated it in his "Yuanhe Junxian Tuzhi (i.e. administrative region annals with relevant atlas appended, Yuanhe denotes the title of Emperor Li Chun's reign in the Tang Dynasty, Junxian denotes the province and county in ancient times county and Tuzhi the annals with relevant atlas appended ") that the Dung denoted "big", implied that with this place based to develop the Western Lands and enjoy great reputation, and so the name of Dunghuang being derived from it. Silk-road, a thoroughfare from the ancient central plains stretched towards the west upon the Chinese ancient silk trade. Both the southern and northern routes of it started from Chang'an (i.e.Xi'an city nowadays) respectively and finally arrived in Dunhuang via Hexi Corridor. Of witch, one route was out of the Yumen Pass, then reached Rome Empire of the day via Qianwangting of Chesshi state, Qiuci state, Shule state, Congling (i.e. Pamir nowadays), Middle Asia and West Asia in turn; the another route was out Yangguan Pass and finally arrived in Rome Empire of the day via LouLan state, Yutian state, Congling (i.e.Pamir nowadays), Darouzhi and Anxi states in turn, total 7000-odd km in whole length.

In the 2nd century B.C., the Emperor Wu of the Han Dynasty twice sent Zhang Qian on a diplomatic mission to the Western Lands, the road to the west was opened thereout which brought convenience to the communication between the Han Dynasty and the Middle Asia than previous times. It, in the meanwhile, improved the friendship between nationalities along the road and promoted the development of human civilization as well.

The trade in a civilized and developed country has the support from the advanced productive forces. Commodities, being involved in the trade contents and the reflection of civilization of a given country, certainly enjoy the high reputation every quarter for its unique use-value. The commodity transaction and circulation help to bring about the formation of the complicated trade route. A good many factors, for example, the geography environment, natural resources, commodity resources, consumption custom of one nationality, aesthetic distance and civilization degree shall influence the formation of traditional trade route. China, the well-known and civilized ancient nation in the world, had ever guided the tide of world civilization in the long historical course, brought his function into play by exporting the ancient civilization via trade routes. The Silk-road, a great international trade route, beat rhythmically and continuously with its characteristics being formed although it had experienced frequent difficulties in history and disturbing of political wind and cloud in those past 2,000 years. The reasons for that are given as follows: firstly, the feudal empires with highly developed productive forces, for instance the Han and Tang dynasties had established in the east as well as Roman Empire in the west. Valuing-trade states, such as Anxi (i.e. Bosi), Dashi (i.e. Arabia) and India, a civilized ancient nation stood between them. A highly developed trade and economical region, starting from ancient China and passing through "two rivers" drainage areas, Araby and Iran altiplano as far as Med region, linked the Eurasia together and established a stable trade relations between what above mentioned in result. The formation of this trade route, as a matter in fact, was the inevitable outcome of the relative equilibrium of the civilization of the east and west. The essence of the traditional trade route is economical chain, which linked together both friendship of people along the Silk-road and the pulsation of economic advance closely. It is recorded in annals that during the period from the 2nd year of Yonghui of the emperor Tang Gaozun's reign (i.e A.D 651) to the 14th year of Zhenyuan of the emperor Tang Dezun's reign (i.e A.D 798), the 37 groups of envoys and trade caravans had been sent to China by Dashi Empire (i.e. Arabia); during previous period of the Tang Dynasty, the Roman Empire, for seven times from a great distance, had sent envoys to offer tributes to the Tang government. Secondly, trade partner supplied what the other needed in accordance with the principle of mutual benefit. The commodities, such as perfumery, medicinal materials, livestock products, glass, jewelry, ivories, fine horses, peltry and wools, together with rare birds and animals, plant seeds such as cotton and purple medic seeds were carried into China via the Silk-road, and in return, Chinese teas, silks, chinas, lacquers, golden and silver household utensils, ironware, and paper making and printing for the west, of which, the silk still held the head and front. Conversely, the traditional trade structure stabilized existence and development of the Silk-road.

The cultural exchange between the east and west became frequent with each passing day along with the prosperous trade along the Silk-road. The Chinese first-class cultural outcomes in the astronomy, medicine, pharmacology, literature, music, and graphics art, etc. were carried into the west in a steady stream and to be used for reference and enriching their spiritual and cultural lives. And the music, dance and acrobatics from both Persia and Eastern Roman Empire, in turn, were introduced into ancient China and their affections to Chinese were profound and lasting.

Chinese scholars figuratively use "the Grant Culture Canal" for the Silk-road appropriately. Along this overland line by which the east and west being linked together, the historical footmarks of Chinese material and spiritual civilization as well as the countless ashes and human marvellous spectacles had been left and contained. It is also regarded as the mirror reflecting the ancient history. The Silk-road provides costful and rich materials for studying the histories relating to politics, economics, community, religions, literatures, arts and relations between ancient China and the West in middle ancient times. It has an important place and unassailable value in studying the histories relating to many subjects. In the Han dynasty, Buddhism, in company with the western art, the Jandhara Buddhist art, music, dance and acrobatics were introduced into ancient China with the result that Chinese original culture kept not a little exotic culture trait. As for the style of Buddha's figure, grottos, temples and pagodas, it, with Chinese traditional architecture skills and engraving mainly based, used culture elements of the Western Lands origin for reference together characterized the Chinese Buddhist art; in the meantime, it also, with feudalistic culture in central plains based, drew on the contents of Indian Buddhist art and had them introduced into the interior in result; and conversely, having the new achievement related to Buddhist art in central plains propagated outwards. Owing to the chronically mutual influence, the mentality of Buddhism, Taoism and Confucianism has been merged into the Chinese grotto art gradually, and resulted in the formation of Chinese unique grotto style with distinctive features in both ideological contents and artistic style. The mural, the important part in the grotto art, directly or indirectly reflected the mutual dealings or connections of various classes, nationalities as well as the Chinese and Western intercourse in certain degree in virtue of artistic refraction because of their contents being on intimate terms with real life. The mural is regarded as the dramatic, visual and historical picture for mirroring the situation of industrial and agricultural economy, wars, religions propagation, people living, social style and features, culture and art, etc. happened during the period of social development.

In ancient times at the latest, the human habitation appeared in Dunhuang Region. The archaeologists had found number of remains of the New Stone Age in Hexi corridor with Dunhuang exactly situating within the distribution of these ancient culture remains. Those remains of long standing, being dotted like stars in the sky and scattered like the pieces on a chessboard, spread all over Dunhuang, for example, never exhausted Crescent-shaped Spring, Mingsha Mountain, Yadan Landform, alias "demoniac town", the Han's Great Wall extended for hundreds of miles, Yangguan Pass which stands guard the entrance to the Western Lands, Yumeng Pass which experiences the history, cloud-kissing White Horse Pagoda, Beacon Tower which stands towering, Dunhuang Old Town which ever being prosperous as well as two Thousand Buddha Grottoes, Yulin Grotto and Mogao Grotto they syncretized the Buddhist art of both the east and west. They make a show of their pride to the world and decorate the splendid history of Dunhuang.

City Gate of Xi'an

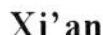

Xi'an

In ancient China of the Han and Tang Dynasties, an international trade thoroughfare, ever binding Central Asia, South Asia, West Asia and others all over the Europe together and bring about enormous influence on developing foreign relations as well, started from Chang'an (i.e.Xi'an city, nowadays), the capital for the both Han and Tang Dynasties, and then went west with large quantities of commodities, particularly the Chinese silk being carried, for this reason, it's called the Silk-road by European historians afterwards.

Eight streams going around and being imperial capitals for dynasties past characterize Chang'an. Xi'an city, being called Chang'an in ancient China, is situated in the west of Guanzhong Plains, leaning against Zhongnan Mountains in the south, looking on Li Mountain the east, leaning close to Mountains and standing at water's side, abundant in all kinds of products, relics and remains, and one of the places where the Chinese ancient civilizations of the Yellow River valley originated, those above mentioned characterize Xi'an city in total. Chang'an had been chosen as the political center in ancient China for 1062 years. Starting from the Western Zhou Dynasty in the 11th B.C to Tang Dynasty, 11 Dynasties made Chang'an their capitals early or later, especially those in the Western Zhou, Qin, Western Han, Sui and Tang Dynasties being very famous. Chang'an took the period of great prosperity in the Tang Dynasty with unprecedented prosperity and the population of more than 800,000 in number. It's not only the national center for both politics and culture, but also the world famous capital and one of important trade bazaars in the world of the day.

In the Han Dynasty, Chang'an city zone covered the area of $36m^2$, the 3 times as large as that of the ancient Rome city of the day. In the emperor SuiWen-di's reign, Daxin city, 10 km to the southeast of original Han's Chang'an city being destroyed in the war and confronted with the threat of Wei river, was built on a large scale, the Tang's Chang'an city was extended upon it. Xi'an, being famous for the history of long-standing, is thought of the place where large quantities of historical relics and remains being assembled. The well-known remains are as follows: Zhouyuan, Western Zhou Feng, Hao capital, E-pang Palace, Han-Tang's Chang'an city and Tang's Daming Palace, etc. The famous ancient mausoleums: Huang Di, QinSshi-huang, Mao (HanWu-di's), Zhao (TangTai-zong's), Qian (TangGao-zong and WuZe-tian's) mausoleums, etc. The namable ancient architectures: Tang's Mig and Small Wild Goose Pagodas, Ming's Bell and Drum Towers, and the city wall of Xi'an, etc. The noted fanes: Xinjiao, Qinglong, Xiangji, Famen, Daxinshan, Caotang Temples and Main Mosque, etc. The shrines in memory of the resolution: Yan'an site, the site of the Eighth Route Army Office in Xi'an, etc. The famous scenic spots: Huashan Mountain and Huaqing Pool, etc. Both Bell and Drum Towers are the symbols of Xi'an whose appearance can be looked out upon by standing on YongNing Gate (i.e.south door), the ancient rampart. If giving a bird's-eye view along the south avenue, a pavilion with antique flavours can be seen which standing over the flow of both heavy traffic and stream of people at the crossroad and showing a moved and magnificent scene. It' s called Bell Tower, the symbol of Xi'an.

In ancient time, both bell and drum were tools to tell the time with the former for daytime and the latter for night in towns all over the country.

Bell Tower, being initially built in the 11th year of Hongwu in the Ming Dynasty (i. e 1384), lies in the center of four comers in Xi'an city nowadays. Being 36m in height, square shape with arched doors at four sides, four spired-corners, wooden architecture with a ladder inside it for going upstairs together characterize it.

Drum Tower, initially being built in the 3rd year of Hongwu of the Ming Dynasty (i. e 1380), just lies about 150m to the west of Bell Tower. Its name comes from a big drum hung within Drum Tower. Rectangle shape, being 34m in height and covering the area of $1842m^2$ for tower body characterize the drum tower where the appearance of the city can be looked into. Its entrance ticket price is the same as that of Bell Tower so that the number of the tourists can be limited and this historical remains be protected as well.

Bell Tower's top takes wooden architecture being enchased with layer of copper inside and then the gold foil outside, with the result that the whole tower looks splendid in green and gold. It's purported that, in those days, both the foundation and tower body were all completed with only a 500kg golden tower top left there. It's too heavy to carry upstairs. The emperor ZhuYuang-zhang (the founder of the Ming country) gave order to put up note in street and said no matter who carried the gold peak on the tower top seat, he could be rewarded the official position and courser discretionarily. Yang, the boss of a liquor workshop saw it and thought it the chance for ChenDa-ting, his counterjumper, to make contribution to the country. He went home and discussed it with ChenDa-ting, and then he accepted the notice.

In the next morning, the emperor ZhuYuang-zhang came to scene in person. ChenDa-ting, holding the gold peak in hands, went upon 108 stairs in number and then put it into the tower pedestal up-rightly, the emperor ZhuYuang-zhang was delighted with it and conferred the title of warlord in Chang'an on him, for this reason, ChenDa-ting was called "Juding HeiHu general " afterward.

In the Tang Dynasty, the empress WuZe-tian gave order to rebuild Drum Tower, after the completion, she banqueted ministers in crowds royally there to celebrate it. DiRen-jie, the Zaixiang (i.e.prime minister in feudal China) reported to the throne that two plaques, in his opinion, should be added together with words of praise "famous scenic spot for both civil and military" on the south plaque, and "giving deafening sound to the universe" on the north one. The empress WuZe-tian was delighted with his words and asked craftsmen to produce plaques with the measure of 10 zhang (unit of length) in length and 2.5 zhang in width for each. No calligraphist within Chang'an city dared to write those large words except for a factotum who was sweeping the street, he, volunteering himself services on the spot, wrote and finished the words with his large besom being dipped in the paint in an instant.

Big Wild Goose Pagoda

7-storied Big Wild Goose Pagoda, 1300-years old, one of famous scenic spots in Xi'an city, was built to store the sutras brought back from India by XuanZhuang, a famous accomplished monk in the Tang Dynasty who designed it himself in accordance with the pattern of India stupa after presenting a memorial to the emperor Tang Gao-zon. It was initially built in the 3rd year of Yonghui of the emperor TangGao-zong's reign (i.e.652), 5 storied in height, and temple's body gradually decayed due to the forested surroundings. It's rebuilt in the 1st year of Chang'an in the Tang Dynasty, 7-storied in total, 64 m in height and it's remained as before with ancient Chinese architectural achievement being revealed richly.

Big Cinen Temple lies at the south end of Xi'an's Yanta Route and originally being called the Wulou Temple in the Sui Dynasty, was rebuilt in the 22nd year of Zhengguan in the Tang Dynasty by Li Zhi, the prince imperial, to commemorate his mother, the empress Wende's"expansive and limitless kindness", and renamed it " Big Cinen Temple" imperially.

Big Wild Goose Temple

The 7-storied Big Wild Goose Pagoda is made of bricks wich wholly substituting for the original mixture of bricks and soils. The Pagoda stands on a foundation of 4m in height, has square outline and the area of 25 m^2 for the first floor, floor-slabs and winding stairs. It amounts to 64m in height with the temple body bricked up jointly and symmetrically, and great momentum as well. It's the masterwork of Chinese Buddhist architectural art. The both steles of "Preface for Tang's Sanzang Shengjiao" written by the emperor TangTai-zong and that of "Notes for Preface of Tang's Sanzang Shengjiao" by the emperor TangGao-zong were inlaid into two sides of the pagoda's south face. ZhuSui-liang, the famous calligraphist in the Eearly Tang Dynasty, copied the epigraph with pretty font.

Both door-head and doorframe of the pagoda were enchased in intaglio with architectural patterns of the Tang Dynasty, sublimity in picture plane and vigorousness in lines. It is important for studying Chinese ancient architectures.

In Big Wild Goose Pagoda, such many degraded officials and celebrities as Tu Fu, Cen Shen, Gao Shi, CguGuang-xi, LiShang-yin and WeiYin-wu, etc. once had their words or verse written on the wall of it. Many of them are excellent works. In the Tang Dynasty, the system of choosing scholars as officials via imperial examinations was in the fashion, of wich, Jinshi exame (the highest imperial examination) was the most difficult, few candidates could pass it. As for those succeeded in the Jinshi exam, they held banquet at Qujiangchi initially being called "Qujiang Banquet", then assembled at Cinen Temple to write superscriptions as the memento. They first wrote it down on a page of graph paper and then elected a representative to write an appended record and inscribed them on the stele in Big Wild Goose Pagoda.

It is said that in the Tang Dynasty, the new one who had past the imperial examination, liked writing superscription on the wall of Big Wild Goose Pagoda. In the time of Shenlong of the emperor Tang Zhong-zong's reign, a Jinshi (a successful candidate in the highest imperial examination) being seized by a whim, inscribed his name on the wall of Big Wild Goose Pagoda, as a result, this contingency was being followed widely, canonized by the imperial family and evolved into "writing superscription on the wall of BigWwild Goose Pagoda". In those days, New Jinshi attended the TanHua Banquet (the Banquet for the number three on imperial examination) held in Qujiang Apricot Garden first, then did boating in Qujiang, went to Cinen Temple and put forward a representative who being proficient in handwriting to write their superscriptions on the wall of Big Wild Goose Pagoda as the memento. No matter who could be in general or prime minister position in future, the aforesaid words on the wall should be rewrite in red. Attending "Qujiang Banquet"and "writing superscription on the wall of Wild Goose Pagoda" became into the way to glory in his distinguished and admirable talent. BaiJu-yi, a famous poet in the Tang Dynasty, had past the imperial examination at his age of 27, wrote the poet of that he was the youngest of Jinshi of the same term, presented his exaggerated glory. This ethos was in popular since the Ming Dynasty, both civilians and successful candidates in the imperial examinations held in Xi'an came to Big Wild Goose Pagoda to write superscription on the wall of it as the memento in succession.

As for the reason of this pagoda being called the " Big Wild Goose Pagoda", in common parlance, the following says can be referred to: sutra story, both wile goose and dove related to the sutra story of Sakyamuni's "bartering meat for dove" were thought of the same congener, and in the Tang Dynasty, the wild goose was treated favour for its propitiousness, as a result, the wild goose was used as the substitute for dove; it's said that in the NalantuoTemple of Indian Hinayana Fane, Buddhist monks, were once very impatient for shortage of meat, one day, they made a joke that Bodhisattva should know they were in shortage of meat while a group of wild gooses were flying over, to their great surprise that the leading goose answered their joke and fell to the ground, these whey-faced Buddhist monks thought it the Bodhisattva and built a high stupa for it, being called "wild goose pagoda", namely the place where Bodhisattva lived; as for various temples in the Western Lands, the first floor of 5-storied Buddhist pagoda takes the shape of a wild goose. So the name of wild goose pagoda comes.

Small Wild Goose Pagoda

15-storied Small Wild Goose Pagoda, built in the 1st year of the emperor TangZhong-zong's reign (i.e.707), being 1300 years old, 45m in height nowadays, known for its cave-in of top, lies inside the Jianfu Temple. The densely covered eaves are taken in its architecture. The unique style, pretty and exquisite workmanship characterize it together. The two Wild Goose Pagodas set off each other to advantage. The arched door-heads of both south and north entrances are enchased with lapidarian weeds, flower patterns and intellectual donor's images, the workmanship is exquisite.

The big wild goose pagoda was not well-known after its being built till the middle period of the Tang Dynasty those who had past the imperial examination (i.e.Jinshi) came here to write their superscription and show their sense of success, namely "writing superscription on the wall of the wild goose pagoda". It, since then, began to come into fashion. In many poems of Tang times, this pagoda was called Cinen Futu (i.e. pagoda) not Wild Goose Pagoda. In the times of the Ming Dynasty, bookmen who had past the provincial examination (i.e.Wenjuren in Chinese) came to Big Wild Goose Pagoda to write superscription to present their elegance in succession, and those successful military candidates (i.e.Wujuren in chinese) came to do the same in the Jianfu Temple, called "writing superscription on the wall of the wild goose pagoda" as well. So both Big Wild Goose Pagoda and small one came forth, the former for Wenjuren and the later for Wujuren to write their superscriptions.

The Jianfu Temple was built on the 100th day after the emperor TangGao-zong' death. To release his soul from purgatory and help him enjoy himself in Pure Land. In Chinese, "Jianfu" is the homophonic of "Xianfu", "Jian" also means mourning over a person's death, namely the Jianfu Temple is the Buddhist rite to save the dead emperor TangGao-zong's soul from suffering. In those days, the Jianfu Temple was the largest temple for imperial family within Chang'an city, the pavilions and superstructures within it being far more magnificent than temples in a general way. Yi Jin, a noted master in the Jianfu Temple, ever went on a pilgrimage for sutras through sea route with Guangzhou the port of sailing. He had past through 30-odd countries and returned with large quantities of sutras together with him, of which, he had translated 230 volumes (56 parts) in total in the Jianfu Temple, and written works of "Nanhai Jigui Biography" and "Biography of Tang Master's pilgrimage for Sutra", etc. These works are important for researching the Buddhist development both at home and abroad.

Small Wild Goose Temple

The iron bell, being cast in the year of 1119, weighed 5000-odd kg and stentorian, is still in existence in the Jianfu Temple. The temple strokes the bell in the morning and the drum at night to remind monks the time to read scriptural passages and tell inhabitants what time it is. Many workshops and handicraftsman are on and off duty by it. The "Wild Goose Pagodas' ding in the morning" is regarded one of "the eight scenic spots in Guanzhong plain" nowadays.

Armored Terracotta Warriors and Horses

Armored Terracotta Warriors and Horses

The discovery of the armored terracotta warriors and horses, being regarded the "one of the great archaeological discoveries in the 20th century" and "the 8th miracle in the world", surprises the world. QinShi-huang Mausoleum, in December of 1987, was listed in the "list of the common cultural heritages in the world" and thereby, become the common and costful wealth for the world.

Local farmers incidentally discovered the Qin's terracotta pit in 1974 when they dug a well. These terracotta being found frequently were "bugbears" in local residents eyes and called the "waren" or "wapen ye" before the pits of Qin's terracotta warriors and horses were discovered. As the story goes that the "bugbear" would appear if farmers dug wells or graves long before. These "bugbears" always raised the devils, made the new grave fallen down suddenly as well as the water in new well exhausted; the "bugbear" sometimes appeared on the well wall abruptly and bulged mouth and goggled at the farmers. In March of 1974, Xi Yang village of Yan zhai community decided to dig eight wells with the 5th well justly located at the southeast corner of No. 1 pit of Qin's terracotta warriors and horses pits. When three or four meters reached in depth, farmers discovered a "wapen ye", they thought it's the ancient temple site under this well and reported it to the leadership. Shanxi province established the leading group in charge of excavating Qin's terracotta warriors and horses pits in QinShi-huang Mausoleum after the approval of National Cultural Relic Bureau. Starting from July 15, 1974, the excavations and studies being involved were carried out on a large scale, and it became the most splendid archaeological work in the last century. After years of trial excavation and drilling, the archaeological staffs had made certain the pit's scope, shape and structure. This great large terracotta pit, having tens of thousands of bronze weapons, 6000-odd pottery figures and horses true to life in it, was named No.1 pit for short because of being found first. At the beginning of 1976,the preparation for the construction of the museum of Qin' terracotta figures of armored warriors and horses was started. The No.1 pit had to be backfilled so that the cultural relics could be protected. The archaeological team took this opportunity to organize relevant groups, by aid of the special tool of Luoyang shovel, to look for new pits around the Qin's Mausoleum. In April 23, 1976, the No.2 pit was found at the spot 20m to the north of No. 1 pit; in May of this year, No. 3 pit was found at the spot 25m to the northwest of the No.1 pit, and an uncompleted earth pit was found between No.2 and No.3 pits with nothing in it as well. The excavation statistics told that 100-odd wooden chariots, hundreds of thousands of bronze weapons, as well as near 8,000 pottery figures and horses similar to life were unearthed at those three pits.

In 1980, two bronze chariots horses unearthed at the west side of Qin's Mau-

Blonze Vehicular Horse

Armored Terracotta Warriors and Horses

soleum have been repaired. Their craftsmanship presented exquisite casting and assembling skills in the Qin Dynasty. The size of them similar to the real ones, lively sense of reality, exquisite material and accuracy characterized them. Their excavation resulted in the shaking of the world. It's to be thought of the great discovery in Chinese archaeological history in late years.

The tomb figure, namely the idol buried with the dead, is the stand-in of slave being buried with the dead. In the both Shang and Western Zhou Dynasties, the institution of burying the living with the dead was in the fashion and being replaced with the tomb figure life-sized along with the collapse of the slave society and foundation of feudal society latterly. The earliest tomb figure being called "chuling" was made of couch grass. Along with the development of productivity, the wood, clay, stone, jade and bronze were used to make tomb figure, together with animal figures and household goods being used as well afterward. The pottery figure had appeared early in New Stone Age though replacing the slave buried with the dead latterly. The pottery had appeared in China 10,000 years ago, the craftspersons gradually were familiar with the mud features and sculpture skills. Early in the Yin Dynasty, the chariot and horses buried with the dead was found, they, together with that found in later period of the Western Zhou Dynasty as well as in the both Han and Qin Dynasties, came down in one continuous line.

The moulding, carving and decoration, torrefaction and colored drawing together constituted the manufacturing process of Qin's terracotta figures of armored warriors and horses. Of which, the first step was to mould unpainted clay idol, then to carve and decorate them carefully, make their passions of pleasure, anger, sorrow and joy stand out. The different parts were given specific moulds and being cemented after carving and decoration. As for the manufacturing the trunk of unpainted coarse clay idol, the way of overlap moulding from bottom to top was taken. The pottery figure was provided with a footstool to stand steadily. The step of colored drawing or pattern came after the exquisite carving and decoration, the paints employed were as follows: vermeil, pink, Chinese date's color, pink and purple, saffron, white, black and ochre, etc. Some clay idols shall be painted before the torrefaction, the other after it. The maximum temperature for torrefying Qin's pottery figures ranged between 1000 and 1050℃, the lower ranged between 950℃ and 1000℃. Solidity in character, uniformity, no seasoning check and distortion together characterized the torrefied pottery figures. The advanced potting craftsmanship in those days thus can be seen.

As recorded in Shi Ji(Historical Records) that more than 700,000 prisoners had built up the Qin's Mausoleum. As for the identities of craftsmen of Qin's pottery figures, the names carved on the Qin's pottery figures can be referred to because the Qin's governor ever asked the craftspersons to carve their names or stamp on the figures they had produced so that the figures quality could be checked and relevant personnel could be accused if the errors happened. This way in old says is called "Wu Qin Gong Ming, Yi Kao Qi Cheng" in Chinese. This happenchance helps the people know the name of these masters.

A Kneeling Armored Terracotta Warriors and Horse

The Buddha's Relics pagoda in Famen Temple

Famen Temple

1700-odd years have past since Famen Temple being initially built in the times of the Huanling's reign in the Eastern Han Dynasty. In the pagoda within Famen Temple, the very rare sutras copied in the Song and Yuan Dynasties as well as the bronze figures of Buddha cast in the Tang, Song, Yang and Ming Dynasties are stored. Famen Temple Museum, facing the south, lies to the west of the pagoda; the Tianzhu palace, the great building in Famen Temple with four huge figures of Buddha 35m tall, lies to the south of the pagoda, vigorously and extensively presents an architecture situation of tripartite confrontation in company with the pagoda and museum there.

1000-odd costful cultural relics, being authenticated the another word-surprising discovery after the Qin's terracotta figures of armored warriors and horses in Qin Mausoleum, were excavated from the largest underground palace within Famen Temple. These very rare treasures occupy the 10 best items of the all. In the meanwhile, the "XuanJi Tu", the remarkable work through the ages, and the story of SongQiao-Jiao going to law relat to the development history of Famen Temple in the past thousands of years. As a result, it's just right to say that the Famen Temple is the treasured pearl along the Silk-road.

Famen Temple took its height of power and splendour in the Tang Dynasty. In the 3rd year of Dali of the emperor Tang Taizong's reign, Famen Temple was honored "Mahatma Buddha's Pagoda". The Buddha's relic stored in the FamenTemple was regarded as the "State-blessed Buddha's relic" with honor or esteem by the Tang's royalty. The emperor issued the imperial order to build large underground palace to store it and develop monks and nuns to a great extent. Famen Temple, from this time on, was promoted to the imperial temple. Temple's field was extended to Huanling Palace with 24 temples in total, being splendid as the imperial court was. The eight emperors, for example the emperor TangGao-zong and empress WuZe-tian, etc. ever opened up the underground palace once 30 years, 6 times in total in Tang Dynasty and greet Buddha's finger relic at Chang'an and Luoyang and attended it with all respect by the emperor. The greeting ceremony was so grand and extravagant that to be regarded the most of all relevant Buddhist religious service. The emperor Yi-zong did his best to hold the extraordinary rite to do it. The details were as follows: "golden curtain as well tender bed, mat made of dragon squamae, mattress made of phoenix feather together with burning chalcedony and using agar cream". It's the busiest and last rite for the Tang Dynasty, even JiaTi-he, the Indian Buddhist monk and a participator of this rite, was presented with a gift of purple cassock by the emperor Xi-zong and returned in glory.

In autumn of 1981, a long spell of wet weather, suddenly a deafening sound gave out, and the old pagoda in Famen Temple collapsed partly soon afterwards with half of it standing upright with pride. In 1986, this pagoda was dismantled and rebuilt. During the cleaning of the ruins, workers found the pagoda foundation of the Ming Dynasty, and the treasure house was found in the later work filled with plenty of treasures.

The 4 finger-bones of Buddha unearthed at the underground palace are the relics of Sakyamuni's real body being authenticate by relevant archaeological excavation, documents and epigraphs, and being thought of the most sacred article for the Buddhist. The specialists said there is only one finger bone is genuine and the only one in the world with the rest being called the "shadow bones" are imitative for the purpose of protecting the real one. The Eight-layer golden Case filled with gold, silver and jade where the Buddha's relic being stored was excavated within the back room of the underground palace. It's decorated with relief, silvers and pearls-inlaid, one layer interlinked another one and being locked up with golden locks.

As for the valuable, splendid and plenty of cultural curiosities excavated in Famen Temple, 121 curiosities, being golden and silver utensils for the oblation in royal court of the Tang Dynasty, are magnificent and exquisitely made; 4000-odd jewelries and jades are exquisitely and dazzlingly carved; and other 16 mystical porcelains, being lost for thousands of years and being authenticated the earliest and finest royal court porcelains, are still fine and glossy in enamel. 13 mei currencies made of hawks-bill shell, the ancient rarest currency founded in the world, were found out among 27000 mei currencies of the Tang Dynasty being cleaned up in the underground palace. The golden and silver tea set there is proved the earliest and highest-grade royal court's tea set in the world, and thus the fact of Japanese tea ceremony being originated from China is testified by this completed practicality. The gilded monk's cane for greeting the real body of Buddha excavated there employs with four sections, 12 rings and 1.96m in length, it's proved the earliest, largest, highest-grade as well as finest instruments used in a Buddhist mass. The gilded and silver case in which the 3rd finger relic of Buddha being emplaced was engraved with gilded picture of nine groups in the diamond-realm mandala, the earliest Mahayana mandala picture founded in the world.

As for the rarity degree of the cultural relics stored in the underground palace, it's difficult to describe them by the word of "invaluable". The large quantities, high grade, completed series, rare and only specy together characterize them. Their values can't be authenticated and evaluated by simple numbers.

Eight-layered Gold Case

Four-doored Gold Tower

Gilded and Silver Utensils in Famen Temple of the Tang Dynasty

Gilded and Silver Utensils in Famen Temple of the Tang Dynasty

Tang's Tri-colored Pottery

Tang's Tri-colored Pottery, a ceramic sculpture, as is well known, "Tri-colors" means many colors, five or seven colors, as many as tens of colors being found from the excavated ceramics of the Tang Dynasty. At the beginning of the twenties of the last century, Longhai Railway was built near Luoyang in Henan province, and as a result, the plenty of Tang's tri-colored potteries and other pottery figures were unearthed at many Tang's tombs and being carried to Pekin, people's attentions, for instance, WangGuo-wei and LuoZheng-yu, etc. the famous scholars, were attracted, foreigners so much as paid high price for them, with the result that the Tang'sTri-colored Pottery, from this time on, become famous all over the cultural relic's circle and the alternative name of colored and glazed potteries produced before the Tang Dynasty.

Tang's Tri-colored Camel Pottery

Tang's Tri-colored Camel Pottery

Tang's Tri-colored Pottery, the generic terms of colored and lead glazed potteries, relevant decorations, grave goods as well as clay sculptures of the Tang Dynasty. Both the historical and the social reason resulted in the appearance of them.

Early in the middle period of the Western Han Dynasty, the earliest lead glazed pottery came into view in Guanzhong plain and being produced largely from that moment. In the Eastern Han Dynasty, they were in production all over the country.

The mass production of both green and brown glazed pottery figures happened to the Northern Wei Dynasty with promoted craftsmanship. The quality of produced lead glazed potteries, as colored ribbons, natural and full, was close to that of the Tang's Tri-colored Pottery. It laid the foundation for the transition of the pottery from being self-colored to being multicolored. The both Sui and Tang Dynasties employed the stagger colored craftsmanship for pottery figures, it, in turn, resulted in a rapid development of this craftsmanship and being closely related to the prosperity in both economy and culture, so much as the social tendency in those days.

As for the diversity of Tang's Tri-colored Pottery, the mould-makings involved are many and varied as follows: the simulative household goods of courtyards, houses, rockeries and ponds in large size; pots, bottles, pans, bowels, the four treasures of the study—writing brush, ink stick, ink slabs and papers, and toys as well in small size; the transportation tools of carriage and ox cart; civil and military officials, warriors, the Hans, foreigners, performing figurines, and leading camel and other character figurines; animal figurines and guard tomb animal figurines. What one expects to find could be produced, it's a feast of eyes. All trades and professionss of the Tang Dynasty are being included.

Maiji Mountain Grottoes

Tianshui

Tianshui, being called Guirongyi (town) in the Zhou Dynasty and set up Shanggui County in the Qin Dynasty and named Qinzhou, Tianshui as well as Chengji in succession, was the transfer station for the Silk-road trade.

Tianshui is known for its multitudinous sweet springs. The noted springs are as follows: Mapo, Guan, Long, Yong as well as Jie springs. Above all, Mapo spring enjoys the most. Tu Fu, a well-known poet in the Tang Dynasty, praised its "water sweeter than milk, and the Buddhist monks in ten directions could be provided with".

Magnificent mountains and rivers as well as the one of the places where the Chinese ancient culture originated from characterize Tianshui. The ancient grottoes, old architectures, tumulus, ancient sites together with old battlefields can be found everywhere. The culture relics for example the FuXi (one of the earliest legendary rulers (2852~2738B.C.) Temple, Maiji Mountain, Xianren Ya (Deva),Shimen, Nanguo Temple, Daxiang Mountain, Yuquan Taoist Temple and Qiu Pond are effulgent. Li Guang, the famous general of the Han Dynasty, was born here, ZhuGe-liang passed through Qi Mountains in Tianshui for six times while doing northern expedition to central plains. ZhangQian passed along Longyou (in Tianshui) while being sent on his mission to the Western Lands, Tang Seng, the famous Buddhist master, ever passed along Tianshui to be on a pilgrimage for Buddhist sutras as well as Tu Fu took refuge at Qingzhou. The above mentioned historical and cultural personalities relate to Tianshui.

The Maiji Mountain, being looked from distance, is celebarated for its unique shape similar to farmer's straw storage pile. The coniform coping in upside, outward central section and the shrink under part together characterize it. A pagoda for the relic of Buddha stands on its top, it results in the loftiness and spectacularity of the Maiji Mountain being surrounded by ridges and peaks, for instance, Tianchi plateau, Xjiangji hill, Douji hill, Sengmao hill and Sanshan Ya, being the same as a upward lotus and out of the ordinary. The Maiji Mountain in company with other two nearby beauty spots of XianrenYa and Shimen are rated as one of the national key beauty and showplaces promulgated by State Department in 1982. Being within them, the scene changes along with the moving steps, all complete in four seasons, for example the bright-colored fresh flowers in spring with butterflies and bees incurred; all trees contend in beauty, abstruse rocks and trees in summer; indistinct misty rain and colored trees can be viewed in autumn; in winter, snow covers pine trees, and all are noble and unsullied. The sceneries there not only in the four seasons but also in the weather of cloudy, sunshine, rain and snow enjoy the diversity respectively. "Maiji misty rain" is the first of Qinzhou eight beauty spots.

The Maiji Mountain lies to the southeast of Tianshui city, 80 li to Qingzhou recorded in ancient books, the former address of Qingzhou does not refer to Tianshui city nowadays. The Maiji Mountain grottoes, a celebrated Buddhism temple on a big scale in history and called Ruiying Temple, are excavated in the long cliff where the excavated grottoes, at a height of 100-odd meters above the ground, spread all over the place be dotted like stars in the sky and scattered like the pieces

on a chessboard, and strew regularly with the plank road built along the cliff and grottoes being linked together. As for excavating majestic grottoes in those days, this topography was selected chiefly. The Maiji Mountain, more than 100 meters in height, is densely covered with pines and cypresses with the pagoda for the relic of Buddha standing on its top as well as the grottoes being seated in the cliff. The mid-cliff collapsed and was being divided into two parts of east cliff and west cliff owing to the earthquakes in the past. The east cliff gives priority to the upper, middle and lower Seven Buddha's Attic. The grottoes and niches in west cliff were excavated before Sui and Tang Dynasties. The plank road was skillfully and steeply built along both east and west cliffs, people are terrified by the sight of them. Buddha's images there are clay sculptures or stone models covered with clay sculpture because of the overcast and rainy climate there (annual rainfall is 840mm, relative humidity is 74%), it resulted in the falling of the great mass of murals with exception of the clay scriptures. As for the grottoes and niches in both east and west cliffs of the mid-cliff ruined by the earthquake happened in both Sui and Tang Dynasty, 194 large or small grottoes and niches had excavated since the 16-States, 7200-odd clay scriptures and stone images as well as the over 1000m² murals are kept in existence. It's one of four noted grottoes of early years in China.

Before the day of Indian Buddhist art being introduced into China, Chinese traditional architecture, sculpture and painting art had been at its height with great achievements. The Maiji Mountain grotto art, based upon the traditional culture since Qin and Han dynasties, is the full Chinese Buddhist art inherited and syncretized the Indian Buddhist art.

The architecture and sculpture as well as nurals constitute the Maiji Mountain Grotto, as is the case for grottoes in other spot. For anyone of them, what above mentioned together with inscriptions, stone tablets and relevant documents characterize them. The murals kept in the Maiji Mountain Grottoes are very rare and some of them supply a gap in painting history though there are a few in number. The murals' contents come down to Buddha, Bodhisattva, Buddhists, Buddha's warrior attendants, donors, as well as relevant Buddhist legends, story of Buddha's previous incarnations, sutra story, the scenes of expounding Buddhist doctrine and Buddha's outgoing, etc. The flexible composition of pictures freely reflects the social situation in those days as well as the craftsmen's subjective dream.

A clay figure known as the Orient Venus

In the times of the 16-States, the murals of the Later Qin and Western Qin State, for the most, are out of existence, as for those only left, they were covered with the murals of the later dynasties. The murals of the Western Wei State, 200-odd m² within more than 40 grottoes, are kept in existence. They are rich in contents, flavor sought; lifelikeness stressed, being well versed in the painting, which in actual existence are excellent works. The Cave 127 keeps the most of murals of the Western Wei State, making up 50% of the total. As to preservative sutra's illustrations kept, to be earliest in time and largest in the area all over the China. The wide scene, tremendous momentum and skillful at painting characterize it, ant to be thought of the curiosity in the world. The murals of the Western Wei State are fresh and mellow in style, graceful and terse in line, natural in the rhythm though few being in actual existence. Many murals of the Northern Zhou State are preserved with diversity in the composition, accurate and vivid modeling, free and vigorous lines, worthwhile shade, fresh and active scene. Of them, the 5 huge "Borousu" Flying Devi murals in the Seven Buddha's Attic are original creations of Maiji Mountain Grotto, and they wrote the new chapter in painting history of the Northern Zhou State. The murals of the Sui Dynasty are harmonious in colors, fresh in style and tone, graceful inartistic conception, unique style and form with spirit combined although few in actual existence. Of a few existed murals of the Tang Dynasty, there are not without representative figure paintings. The Ming Dynasty murals enjoy the majority of those in actual existence, garish colors, numerous style characterize them, but no lack of fine works.

Steel Bridge over the Yellow River in Lanzhou

Lanzhou

Lanzhou, alias Jincheng, as the story goes that the EmperorWu granted it for a big gold to be gained here on his way to do western expedition. Narrow corridor, Gaolan Mountain standing at the south and the White Pagoda Mountain at the north with the Yellow River passing between them as well as the key-point at the Silk-road together characterize it. As for its importance of strategic passage, it's the key pass and strongpoint along the Silk-road being called Jincheng Pass in history, and ever played important role in resisting the foreign aggression for an unobstructed Silk-road. Jincheng Pass originally situated in the west of the piedmont of White Pagoda Mountain, north of Lanzhou city nowadays, was demolished in 1942, and became a residential area now. People in Lanzhou city, at the mention of Jincheng Pass, know its exact location, but it is a pity, this location only refers to Jincheng Pass initially built in the Song Dynasty and lasted until the Yuan, Ming as well as the Qing Dynasties, not that before the Tang Dynasty. "YuHe's land charts &annals of prefectures and counties"(YuHe: the title of Emperor Li Chun's reign in Tang Dynasty, A.D806~820) recorded that Jincheng Pass originally being situated in the west of state town, and EmperorWui in the Zhou Dynasty had set up Jinchengjin and then renamed Jincheng Pass in the 18th year of Kaihuang(i.e.A.D.598) in the Sui Dynasty. "Jin" means "crossing" in Chinese. The Jincheng Pass should be built at the crossing of the Yellow River. As to the records in item of "Wuquan County in Lanzhou state" in "TaiPinHuanYuJi", the JinchengPass lay to the southwest of Jincheng prefecture and near the river. Wuquan

County was the seat of Jincheng Prefecture. Two books give different answers to the question of where the JinchengPass's site is. No words said that JinchengPass was situated in the north of the Yellow River.

As to the location of Jincheng Pass in the Tang Dynasty, the Jincheng Post of the day should be mentiond first. As the "Tang's six institutions •Shangshu-Bingbu•JiabuLangzhong"(Shangshu-Bingbu:high official of Department of War; Jiabu:the title of office; Langzhong: official in feudal China) goes that "A post being set up for per 30 miles" on the road to the west. In the Tang Dynasty, a road starting from Chang'an went west till Lintao area, then went to Lanzhou through Again valley, successively crossed the Yellow River from Hekou crossing and went to Yongdeng, finally went west from Wuwei area. It's just the road (i.e.post road) for CenShen, a famous poet, to go west (page 306, Gansu's Ancient History). Hekou crossing was centuries-old. Jincheng Pass came from Jinchengjin (crossing), the posthouse should share the same place with the crossing or near it. Accordingly, that Hekou area is the site of Jincheng Pass. It's coincident with the relevant records in both "YuHe's land charts &annals of Prefectures and Counties" and "TaiPinHuanYuJi". Pass, in ancient times, was the place to levy taxes upon those in and out. "posthouse" was the place for officials, common people as well as the businessmen and travelers to rest. According to Tang's rule, Pass took three grades of upper, middle and lower grades. The upper grade referred to the Pass being set up around the capital and being situated in the post road; those along the post road and those around the capital but away from the post road pertained to the middle grade; and the rest pertained to the lower grade(refer to "Tang's six institutions" and "Jiu Tang Shu (Old History of the Tang Dynasty) • official title" for more detains). As for the Jincheng Pass pertained to the middle grade, it's a pity that no relevant records can be found in "Tang's six institutions" though being set up before the completion of this book.

Hecou area, situated at the foot of hills and by the side of the Yellow River, enjoyed the favorable conditions for building the post house. The post road went along the hills as stated in the poem of "post road going along the foot of hills" and "water swashing the town wall", here the town wall, that is to say, referred to that of Pass rather than Lanzhou town. This Pass stood aside the Yellow River, as a result, the wall was swashed by the water. As recorded in "YuHe's land charts & annals of prefectures and counties", Lanzhou town lay at 20 li to the Yellow River, the river water could not flow along side of it, let alone swashing the town wall. No town ever was situated at the north of the Yellow River of the day, as regards the post house, it only had courtyard wall. What the poet only mentioned were tall building, foot of hills, courtyard, trees, garden and "river water swashing the town wall" with exception of the scenery in prefecture town, they differed with those mentioned in Gao Shi's

Lanzhou

Waterwheel on the Yellow River

The Mother on the Yellow River

poem "looking clear west by going upstairs, mountains and rivers joining and occupying eyes, rapids giving whistle liking flying arrows, crescent hanging over the tower just liking a bow." In this poem, the poet mentioned the BaiMa Lang" within the Yellow River nowadays. This proved that tall building in post house was not in the north of the Yellow River in Lanzhou Prefecture town. If the Jincheng Post being situated at the foot of the White Pagoda Mountain, the post road would go through the Prefecture town, it's impossible, by the book, in those days, much less to set up post house within the town. As for those within the town originally, they were moved outside the town latterly.

The Northern Song Dynasty built Jingcheng Pass, the first time for Jingcheng Pass, on the north bank of the Yellow River for a reason of military affairs. Jingcheng Pass of the both Sui and Tang Dynasties was located at the west of Lanzhou town. They differed in their locations.

The White Pagoda Mountain

Sheepskin Raft

Sheepskin Raft, a centuries-old and simple ferry for both passengers and freights, also called "leather boat" made of cowskin or sheepskin, an old tradition but still prevails in the Hui, Han, Baoan, Dongxiang, Sala as well as the Tu nationalities lived along the bank of the Yellow River within Qinhai, Gansu and Ningxia churchyards. Lanzhou area enjoys the majority.

The Jincheng crossing, being built early before the Western Han Dynasty, employed the Sheepskin Raft for passengers and freights. In the year of 81 B.C., the Western Han government set up Jincheng Prefecture with its office seat situated in Yunwu and 13 counties under its jurisdiction, of which, the Jincheng county seat situated in Xigu district, lanzhou city nowadays (lanzhou urban district pertains to its domination in those days). The ancient Jincheng crossing was on the bank of the Yellow River in Xigu district nowadays. In the year of 50B.C., Zhaochong-guo, the general of the Western Han Dynasty led troops to cross the Yellow River here for many times and to resist the Hun troops and battle against Xiqiang nationality (refer to Hanshu•Zhaochong-guo Biography for more details). As stated in "Three Kingdoms (Wei, Shu Han and Wu) Rrecords" that Jiang Wei, the famous general of Shu Han state, ever laid siege to Didao while doing the northern expedition against Wei state in the year of A.D. 3, Wei's reinforcements crossed the Yellow River to rescue Didao from Jincheng crossing. In the year of A.D.553, the emperor Tai-zu of the Northern Zhu state led tens of thousands of cavalrymen to go west through Jincheng crossing (refer to Zhou book• Tai-zu Records for more details). Many records related to the Sheepskin Raft can be found from historical documents. As mentioned in "Shui Jing Zhu (Commentary on the Waterways Classics)•YeYuiShui Section" that in the 23rd year of Jianwu in the Han Dynasty, the emperor ever sent troops to cross the river from south bank by "leather boat" (Sheepskin Raft)". As recorded in "old Tang Book• East Female State Biography" that "going over the river by cowskin raft"; as recoded in the "TaiYangYinJing•Weapon Section• Appliance for Crossing Streams" that "going over the river by help of the air swim bladder made of sheepskin with its air holes frapped tightly and the bladder under the person's body". Thus it can be seen that Sheepskin Raft prevails for centuries.

Sheepskin Raft, small in shape and simple in structure as well as light in deadweight, can hold freights of more than one thousands of kilograms, and gives priority to carry passengers and concurrently holds freights with only one driver. It's easy to navigate on the Yellow River and manufacture. Firstly, to bind up a quadrate raft frame, 2 m in width, 3m in length and with small panes within it, with tens of crabsticks of a diameter of 3 or 4 centimeters; and then to secure the frame with a rope, cord, or chain; finally, to lash 10-odd air swim bladders made of sheepskin down to the frame in order. The relevant historical scenes happened to this age-old river will come into your eyes while rafts assemble on the Yellow River. Sheepskin Raft not only serves the passengers and freights but also becomes the view out of the common along the Yellow River.

Sheepskin Raft on the Yellow River

Huanghe Stegodon, unearthed at Heshui county, is a fossil in the early period of the Pleistocene Epoch, more than two million years ago

Huanghe Stegodon

The Huanghe Stegodon, unearthed at Muqi village, Banqiao countryside, Heshui County in Gansu province and being the most earliest, completed and biggest stegodon fossil in the world, is named the Huanghe Stegodon by both biologist and archaeologist.

Huanghe Stegodon, being carefully glued together, reinforced, put up as well as being recovered with 8m in length, 4 m in height and 3.2m for its tusks, and being stored in Pekin Natural Museum, is the real emersion of old life-form before the historical records. The Huanghe Stegodon is generally deduced the Stegodon of about 100 years old from its concrescence degree of the skull, pelvis shape in company with the situation of the teeth growth and abrasion, and being buried by mud and sands owing to its false step early before 2～3 million years after comparing the strata and commensal vertebrate fossils. As early as in the period of the Pleistocene Epoch, 1～3 million years ago, both the North and South all over the China enjoyed temperate and humidity climate even though in the later period of the Pleistocene Epoch. Both old oriental Stegodon and Stegodon lived in times of the Pliocene to the Pleistocene. The torrid and semi-torrid zone, gentle terrain, hot climate, rich rain, large quantities of rivers and lakes together with distributed grasslands characterized the Longdong region in Gansu in those days where the Huanghe Stegodons, as alike as African elephants, lived in groups on leaves, branches, even the tender trunks and roots; their long and strong front teeth were the best weapon to resist invaders. Subsequently, with the crustal movement, sudden changes happened to the natural environment in the Yellow River valley and the good and bad were all properly placed and provided for, the Huanghe Stegodons became extinct and disappeared.

The nowadays Longdong's natural environment greatly differs with that when Huanghe Stegodons lived. The former rivers, lakes and fields have already be changed into the base of Loess Plateau with Longdong's remains to be most telling witness of the sea being changed into the mulberry fields and mulberry fields into the sea. Their fossils become the lively teaching materials to guess the changes in the natural world in ancient times. The Huanghe Stegodon dumbly pours out the vicissitudes related to the globe, and in the meantime becomes the rare material for researching the geological climate of that time.

Scenery at Bingling Grotto

Bingling Temple Grotto

Binglin Temple, at about 35 km to the southwest of Yongjing county town, is situated on the north bank of the Yellow River. As recorded in Vol.4 of "Hezhou Annals" that "Bingling Temple standing at 60li to the north of Hezhou town, bordering on the upper air, overlooking the Yellow River, carving the Buddha figures out of the mountain stone with 10-odd zhang (unit of length) in height for horizontal figures and a few zhang in length for recumbent ones, each 8 caves for upper, middle and lower layers with colored Buddha figures within them; the sandalwood and different herbal medicines are produced here, abundant springs spray, and gladden the hearts. In summer's first month and August, people near foreign countries and nationalities visit here and to be known as the old relic of the Tang Dynasty. The censor of the Ming Dynasty ever erected a monument where "The first wonder in the world" being inscribed to glorify it. Bingling Temple Grotto, one of the celebrated Buddhist grottoes, Buddhist culture center in Hehuang Region along the south route of the Silk-road as well as one of grotto temples of being earliest influenced by the Indian Buddhist art, are regarded as the Six Great Buddhist Grottoes in company with Dunhuang Maogao Grotto, Yungang Cave, Longmen Grotto, Maiji Mountain Grotto and Xinjiang Kezer Grotto in China.

The excavation of Bingling Temple Grotto can be dated back to the early Jin Dynasty. As recorded in "Fuhan Linhe Tangshu Valley Temple", the Vol.52 of "Fa YuanZhuling" written by ShiDao-xuan in theTang Dynasty that "early in the Jin Dynasty, Tangshu valley situated at 50 li to the west of Hezhou town, covered with immense forest. Looking south by the mountaintop, Jishi mountains, being the polar region where DaYu ever led and controlled the water, could be found, where ridges and peaks rising competitively and widely different as it were Buddhist pagoda or storied building; pines, cypresses and rocks set off each other and presented the red and cyan colors, being extraordinary as it done by the Creator; Tangshu valley situated at 20li to the south of Jishi Mountains, where Buddhist monks excavated the mountains to build temple, made the bridge over the river, planted melon, fruit and vegetables around the temple. A stone door bordered on the river was inscribed on words "Being built in the year of Taishu in Jin Dynasty". In the eastern valley of the temple, another temple suspended in midair, the ding could be heard as well as foreign monks be seen regularly but the undoubted location couldn't be found, as a result, being entitled the name of Tangshu valley, namely the devas. All those entered into the Jishi Mountain whould become enrapt and sometimes find the temple and monks emerging from the clods. The sweet and limpidity spring water out-flew from both eastern and western mountains would make drinkers live

Big Buddha, Bingling Temple Grottoes, Cave 171

forever". The above mentioned tells that monks ever lived here early in the Jin Dynasty. The grotto shape resembles that of Yungang and Longmeng grottoes. The pagoda-shaped niches are the exclusive. Sculptures and murals within it concentratedly reflect the artistic features of Bingling Temple Grotto.

Bingling Temple Grotto takes 694 stone images and 82clay sculptures. Powerful Buddha's images, slender and graceful ones of Bodhisattvas employ every elegant mien. The hugest Buddha's image is 30m tall, sitting in a shapely posture, fluent in clothes' line as well as solemn and respectful in manner characterize it, it can compare beauty with Leshan Huge Buddha Figure. As regards sculptures of the Tang Dynasty in Cave 64, Bodhisattva's two forms stand with slight sideways at both sides. Holding long eyebrows, lunate eyes, soulful smile and putting the palms together characterize Bodhisattva; the one form holds her wiggly and graceful body with one hand slightly holding up flower; the another form holds water bottle in nutant hand, they are vividly depicted. Buddha's image is centered in the Cave 64. He deplores the condition of the world and pities for the fate of people solemnly and respectfully. Their looks stand in vivid contrast against each other.

Bingling Temple Grotto takes over 900m² murals. Precise in composition of the pictures, compendious in lines and floweriness color characterize them. Sutra stories are involved in the murals contents. For example the mural in Cave169, the female donor takes double coiled buns, drooping hairs, slightly drifting streamers and myriads of manners and being accompanied with the inscription of "Being built in March 24 of the 1st year of Jianhong", the earliest ink inscription found in China up to the present. It testifies that grottoes within Bingling Temple were excavated early in A.D.420, after this, the grottoes of the Northern Wei, Northern Zhou as well as the Sui, Tang, Song, Yuan, Ming and Qing Dynasties can be found here. 212 grottoes, 700-odd figures as well as near 50 sculptures in relief are kept in actual existence there which can be divided into three zones as follows: lower temple zone, caves zone and upper temple zone. The figure appeared in many articles only refers to the grottoes in the lower temple zone where the lower temple, Dayageng, Zendo, Shuilian Hole, Laojun Cave, Yejigou, Baitagou and Foyetai are included. A distance of 1.5km exists between lower temple and caves zones and about 3km between the lower temple and the upper temple zones where the grottoes distribute dispersedly. The figure of grottoes in Bingling Temple should include all grottoes and niches within those three zones. The final statistical figures are as follows: 191 grottoes exist within the lower temple zone, 8 grottoes within the caves zone and 13 grottoes within the upper temple zone, 212 grottoes in total. There is a forest of peaks and ridges around the Bingling Temple, ravines distribute in length and breadth. Any other grottoes and niches perhaps can be found in gullies and valleys in future.

Bingling Temple Grottoes, Cave 169, the Western Qin Dynasty, Mural Painting

Bronze Galloping Horse

The academia-shaking and unrivalled Bronze Galloping Horse, 45cm in length, 10.1cm in width and 34.5cm in total height, unearthed at a General Zhang's tomb in leitai, Wuwei city, exhibited both at home and abroad for many times, enjoys the high prestige of the world and to be thought of the elaborate work among fine and marvelous cultural relics stored in Gansu provincial museum. Many people are fond of and think no end of it which enjoying pet names of "Mata feiyan", "Mata Feiniao", "Tiama" as well as " Machao Longque". It's causative of being chosen as the Chinese Tour Symbol from thousands upon thousands of cultural relics.

Bronze Galloping Horse of the Eastern Han Dynasty, unearthed at Guleitai, Wuwei

The unique Bronze Galloping Horse, in 1996, was authenticated the national grade cultural relic by National Cultural Relics A-Bureau. It's rare for its higher values in art, science and historical research. As to its many pet names, "Mata feiyan" is just right, the reasons are as follows: ShenYue in the ancient Southern Dynasty, the emperor Jian in the Liang State and XieLing-yong, etc. respectively compared "Feiyan(flying swallow)" to "Courser" in their poems; another example is that ancient people liked to name a courser the "Ziyan(purple swallow)"; as stated in the poem "Seven lives" wrote by ZhangXie who called the"Feiyan"and "Courser" simultaneously; the first sentence in the poem "Praising" wrote by LiShi-min and related to the "six coursers of Zhao Mausoleum" mentioned "ZiyanChaoyue"; most of all, the poem "HuiyinXing" wrote by XieLing-yong being noted and cited by LiShan in his "Xijing Miscellanea" that the emperor Wen of the Han Dynasty had nigh coursers, one called "FeiyanChaoliu". The Bronze Galloping Horse's shape and structure are as consistent with that of "Feiyanliu" or"ZiyanChaoyue".

The Bronze Galloping Horse's modeling closes to characteristics of the swift horse described in "scripture related to looking at a horse to judge its worth", the details are as follows: small and square-built horse's head, big and bright eyes, small ears and big nose, gentle underlip and steep and square-built muffle, powerful and square-backed horseback, wide and patulous thorax, round knee as well as thin and long legs. Thus it can be seen that this bronze horse being molded after consulting the coursers of that time. The Han Dynast thought much of raising horses. Many bronze courser models were molded for selecting and breeding horses, for example, both emperor Wu in Western Han Dynasty and MaYuan in the Eastern Han Dynasty ever had molded bronze course models. The Gansu corridor, from of old, is one of the important horse lands; MaYuan held a post in Gansu area for years and his courser model was best-known and being imitated naturally. Here stressing the fact that both Bronze Galloping Horse and courser model mainly based upon the coursers lived in Gansu corridor which were the breed varieties of being improved and controlled mating with fine horses from Chinese Qinghai-Tibet Plateau, Wuxun and Rouzhi States in the Western Lands and Dawan State in Central Asia for generations. They could pull in front of a chariot and to be ridden. The followings give causes for it: Gansu area, especially in Liangzhou region, people there became rich and existed on raising horses and bred coursers; as recorded in "Han Shu• Emperor Wu Record" that "in the spring of the 4th year of

Bronze Carts, unearthed at Guleitai Wuwei, The Eastern Han Dynasty

Yuanding in the Western Han Dynasty, the courser appeared in Wuwa Pool(i.e. the place in Dunhuang region,and the nomadic land for Wuxun and Rouzhi people) and neighed like a heavenly steed soaring across the skies"; the name "Tianma" just comes of it. In the Han Dynasty, only the breed of Dunhuang horse, Wuxun horse from Yili region and Dawan horse were so laureled. Secondly, the Dawan horses were carried into ancient China for many times after the emperor Wu's successful expedition to Dawan State. As recorded in "Shi Ji(Historical Records)• Dawan Biographies" that the emperor was fond of Dawan horses, the envoys in an endless stream sent horses to the emperor, they could be seen as many as 10 groups, as little as 5or 6 groups within one year. Most of these Dawan horses were pastured in Hexi corridor, the necessary way for Dawan horses being sent to the Hang Dynasty and fine pasturages could be provided there. Thirdly, as recorded in "Sanfu Huangtu" that the bronze model of the courser, being set up in front of Jingma door where the eunuch office situated, based on the Dawan horse, and "Jingma door" came of it. Finally, pulling carts, ridding and good adaptabilities characterize the ancient horse, the outstanding virtues of Dawan horses were rapid in action. The breed variety of being improved and controlled mating with each other would combine the features of Chinese horse and Dawan horse.

As for the Han's Bronze Galloping Horse and those bronze horses being excavated within Gansu province, The magnificent in physique, wide and deep thorax, square-backed and short horseback, correctitude buttocks, brawniness, tall and big dobbin, small head and ears, big eyes, gracile and bendy neck(similar to crane's neck), spindlelegs, clear in arthral muscles and tendons as well higher tailbone together characterize the war horse. In conclusion, the Bronze Galloping Horse is the outcome of cultural, artistic and fine breed exchanged between China and foreign countries.

To whinny and gallop with its head and long tail raising leftwards, three horse's hooves emptying out and right posterior hoof treading on a flying swallow who spreading the wings and looking back alarmedly, round-eyed, long swallow tail without forfication. Their match is excellent and incomparable. The horse gallops than flying swallow does which being frighten by horse's invincible might,; the flying swallow, in turn, flutters and flies in full charge similarly to sparrow hawk and does not show the impression of weakness to "Tianma", just like an competition for supremacy which surpasses the space-time.

Great Buddha Temple in Zhangye

Great Buddha Temple in Zhangye

In the 6th year of Tiansheng in Song Ren-zong's reign (i. e.1028), the Western Xia Regime made a raid on Huihu tribe and took Ganzhou by storm. As of the 3rd year of Jingyou in the Song Dynasty (i.e.1036, the 3rd year of Guangyun in the Western Xia Regime), the Western Xia Regime occupied the whole Hexi corridor. Next year, YuanHao, the king of the Western Xia Regime, promoted Suzhou to Fanhejun, Ganzhou to Zhengyijun and in the meanwhile set up Huanhua Fu there as well as the Western Liang Fu in Liangzhou. YuanHao carried out a series of policies similar to that of Han's regime to manage and develop Hexi region. In LiQian-shun's reign, the state was at the height of power and splendor, widely translating sutras and building temples were important measures to administrate various matters of Hexi region. Both Huguo Temple in Liangzhou and Great BuddhaTemple in Zhangye were established under this historical background.

As to the date that Zhangye's Great Buddha Temple being set up, the "Chici Baojue temple Record"(i.e. the tablet-inscription related to establishing Baojue temple being granted and ordered imperially) written in the 2nd year of Xuande in the Ming Dynasty (i.e.1427) recorded that Zhangye's Great Buddha Temple was initially built in the time of LiQian-shun's reign. As stated in the inscriptions on a bronze tablet, being produced in the 13th year of Chenghua in the Ming Dynasty (i. e.1477) and excavated at the stomach of horizontal Buddha figure, that Zhangye's Great Buddha Temple was initially established by the Western Xia Regime in the 1st year of Yong kang of the Emperor LiQian-shun's reign. As recorded in the inscriptions on another bronze tablet related to rebuilding HongrenTemple in the 12th year of Qianlong in the Qing Dynasty (i.e.1747) and excavated at the stomach of horizontal Buddha figure as well, that Zhangye's Great Buddha Temple was initially established in the 1st year of Yong kang in the Jing Dynasty. The textual research tells that "Yong'an" was the title of LiQian-shun's reign, not " Yongkang". To comprehensively analyze the relevant records in both "Gansu's towns Annals" compiled in the 14th year of the emperor QingShun-di's reign and "Ganzhou prefectural government Annals" edited in the 44th year of the emperor QingQian-long's reign, the records of Zhangye's Great Buddha Temple being initially built in the 1st year of Yong'an of the Western Xia Regime (i.e.1098) " is without fail, those records in the inscriptions of "being built in the 1st year of Yongkang" is error.

With regard to establishment of the Zhangye's Great Buddha Temple, the legendry records in annals say that "in the times of LiQian-shun's reign, a Buddhist monk Wei, his surname, and Si Neng, the name in religion, formally acknowledged YanDan, the state master, as his teacher to study significant Buddhist doctrine and real truth, and became a highly skilled and wise man after a more advanced course of study, with the result that all people within the territory idolized and revered him, and called him the state master. One day, he restrained himself and sat quietly, suddenly he perceived an auspicious sign, and the sapiential light appeared brightly. He stood up and looked around but nothing could be seen, he traced the light and came to the spot where the light disappeared and dug a hole one foot deep, a jade green tile was found underground, then he continued another three feet deep and finally a found a golden brick with ancient nirvana Buddha statue under it. He perceived that he was doomed to be the Buddhist. He felt an upsurge of emotion and vowed to build a great temple to make offerings to Buddha. He, within the scheduled time, finished this grand temple with four corners looking up the far distance, just like a great bag. As stated in "Chici Baojue temple Record" that in the time to mold the Buddha figure lain on his side, the highly skilled craftsmen finished it cautiously and conscientiously at the second month after the completion of the temple. 5 years, commencing on the 1st year of Yongan and ending in the 3rd year of Zhenguan in the Western Xia Regime (i.e.1103), were spent to build this Great Buddha Temple. The temple was initially called "Kasyapa Buddha Temple", alias "Wofo" Temple called with all respects by common people owing to Sakyamuni's nirvana statue there. The original Wanshou Jinta Temple and Gianying Temple lie to the north and south of "Wofo" Temple respectively. Both of them assume the crisscross after crossing with axes of "Wofo" Temple. They were called "cross temple" for short in the Song, Yuan and Ming Dynasties. As for the legend of that empress Liang of the Western Xia Regime had ever set up

Inside the temple lies a statue of Sakyamuni in 34.5m long, the biggest indoor Reclining Buddha in the country

Wood Tower in Zhangye,constructed in the Sui Dynasty(582 A.D.)

the rite here to save the souls of the dead after the setting up of Zhangye's Great Buddha Temple, no historical record to refer to.

The collection of Buddhist sutras in Zhangye's Great Buddha Temple in the Ming Dynasty showed its full prosperities. Early in the times of Yongle in the Ming Dynasty, many rare Buddhist sutras of both palace edition and a few of GuSu workshop's block-printed edition were collected there. In the 5th year of Zhengtong of the emperor MingYin-zong's reign (i.e.1440), the "Ming's SanZang ShenJiao Bei cang", the block-printed edition and being used for conferring the title upon famous mountains and great temples, was finished in Pekin. Later, Daoshen, the great master and the imperial envoy sent to give sermon, bestow Buddhist treasures on Zhangye's Great Buddha Temple and be in charge of the handing over, teaching and management of accompanied Buddhist sutras in succession and other matters concerned. The "SanZang canon" sutra consists of 1621 parts of 6361 volumes being packed within 636 cases. They, starting from the 6th year of Zhengtong to the 10th year of that in the Ming Dynasty, 10 years in total, were carried to Zhangye's Great Buddha Temple, after that, the ceremony of accepting imperial edict issued on Dec. 15, the 10th year of Zhengtong in the Ming Dynasty was hold with respect. The detailed contents of it are as follows: "Respectful emperor thinks so much of the people that he confers the "SanZang canon". One of "SanZang canon" would bestow on Ganzhou's "Wofo" Temple for keeping forever and for monks to read with all respects and pray blessings for both the country and people. They should be well collected with respects against being lent privately, sacrilege and damages. Those who violates it will be mercilessly punished".

The Ming government thought much of the Buddhist culture, especially the"SanZang canon" being conferred on Zhangye's Great Buddha Temple by the emperor MingYin-zong, they accelerated the prosperity and development of Buddhism there.

As regards the construction of collected sutras in Zhangye's Great Buddha Temple, the sutra's sculpture and printing were much concerned except for repairing and replenishing part of them. As early as the time that Zhangye's Great Buddha Temple contacted Wuwei's Luoshi Temple for replenishing sutras, the technical personnel being adept at engraving were imported. As a result of it, near 1000 engravings related to the sutra and joss were accomplished for printing from the time of the 10th year of the emperor QingShun-zhi's reign to the period of the emperor QingQian-long's reign. These engravings, together with "Beicang" sutra conferred by the emperor MingYin-zong and Wanshou golden tower were regarded as magic weapons for guarding the temple.

Zhangye's Great Buddha Temple, centuries-old, has experienced historical changes, where the Chinese biggest indoor recumbent Sakyamuni statue being clay-molded, the integrated Ming's "Beicang"sutra as well as large quantities of rare Buddhist cultural relics and documents are saved. It's not only the showplace of golden Zhangye, being an importanta town along the Silk-road, but also the place to study the Buddhist culture.

Music-playing Chart

Painted Bricks in Jiuquan Han's Graves

Rich and colorful as well as bright-colored characterizes the painted bricks in Jiuquan Han's graves. As regards the shape and structure of the graves, the quadrate coffin chamber with a sloped tunnel in the front of the door of it. The graves, because of the differences in their construction materials, are arranged under categories of arched brick graves, graves combined bricks and adobes, a few tombs as well as small bricking graves and coffins for the old dead, five in total. Most of them face to east, few to the south. As for the shape and structure of Jiuquan Han's graves, they are arranged under categories of the grave with a single quadrate, bricking chamber and an arched bricking door; the grave with a single chamber combined bricks and adobes; the grave with front and back chambers, arched bricking vault; the child's grave with bricking pit chamber. Tunnel, door, corridor, front and back bricking chambers constituted the grave's shape and structure in the latter stage of the Eastern Han Dynasty. The cultural relics such as wares, bronze wares, bone wares, silks as well as painted bricks and murals were unearthed at Han's graves. The content of over 300 painted bricks touch upon the politics, military affairs, economy as well as the culture and living, etc. The judgment from the facts tells that 1400-odd ancient graves being widely distributed in the circumference of 10 km around. JiayuGuan, under the jurisdiction of Jiuquan prefecture in both the Han and Wei Dynasties, enjoyed the prosperity of "lots of envoys coming and going", "merchants and peddleries both at home and abroad staying or passing the frontier fortress every day", as a result of it, abundant cultural heritages were left.

Ploughing Chart

The figures on Han's painted bricks were depicted vividly, strikingly true to life, the colorful social life in those days was reflected and to be regarded as the vivid portrayal of people's lives then and there. The general appearances of the painted bricks are arranged under categories of ① stationing troops to open up wasteland. In the Han Dynasty, the garrison troops should open up wasteland and grow food grain concurrently. As painted on "Chart of Station Troops Opening up Wasteland" that some soldiers dressing the ranks and going into military training with spears and shields led by military officers; some doing soil preparation, planting and threshing grains on the ground, the farmwives also can be seen in the scene. Most contents of painted brick relate to the station troops opening up wasteland owing to both Jiuquan and JiayuGuan closing to the frontier area in those days;②dak. The post-horse was mainly engaged in the military communication in ancient time. The chart of "Estafette Inform" was depicted vividly to the life. It not only reflects the military communication in those days but also provides the reference for researching the development history of Chinese ancient post;③ hunting. The wasteland between Jiuquan and JiayuGuan in old time had various species of animals there. The contents of painted bricks relate to hunting, shooting wild pigs, hawking and pursuing conies. The animals deal with oxen, sheep, horses, chooks, dogs and pigs, etc;④kitchen work. The interesting and characteristic cooking scenes, for example preparing a meal, cooking fire, shouldering water, cutting meat as well as roasting meat and cooking wheaten food, etc. look familiar; ⑤ military affairs. The Hexi region was important place stationed by huge forces since the Han Dynasty. The chart of tour of military inspection emerges the vast and mighty scene of going out for a battle and tour of inspection in those days. The huge barracks and the enclosing walls as well as the tents are witness of garrisoning troops there;⑥sericiculture. The painted bricks employed the picturesque scenes of picking mulberry-leaves, sericiculture as well as reeling the silk thread off cocoons;⑦entertainments. The remarkable dance scene, such as "Ta-ge (singing and dancing at once)" and "three dancers" dance expresses their elegancy actions and impassioned ambience. In conclusion, all aspects of the life in those days were involved in the contents of painted bricks, people seem to be personally on the scene and return the old days while seeing them. They are detailed and dependable materials for researching the history of that time.

Sheep-slaughtering Chart

Ox-slaughtering Chart

Jiayu Pass

As the common saying goes that the Great Wall starting from Sanhai Pass in the east and ending at Jiayu Pass in the west. Jiayu Pass, known as the impregnable Pass in the world, is regarded as the end-point of the Great Wall and the strategic passage of the Silk-road though it missed the Silver Age of interchange of the economy and culture between the east and the west along the Silk-road. The site selection of it proved the importance of this place in history.

The existent Jiayu Pass tower, in the 5th year of Hongwu in the Ming Dynasty (i.e. 1372), initially was built by Feng Shen, a high-ranking military officer in charge of going on a punitive expedition to non-Han nationalities lived in Hexi region, who selected the slope field northwest of "Jiuyan Spring" to build earth castte and set up the pass there. "Jiuyan Spring", alias the "Mountain Spring Flowing Water" in old days, a limpidity and perennial spring being regarded as one of "eight landscapes in Suzhou". As recorded in "Qing's Border District Record Outline" that "Pass's construction basing upon the wellhead, then the city tower and the Great Wall following hard after the Pass in succession and the Pass can be defended safely after the Great Wall being accomplished." The Pass circumvallation is 733.3m in perimeter, 11.7m in height and covers the area of 33500-odd m^2. The eastern city gate called "Guanghua Men" and the western "Rouyuan Men" are inside the Pass city. The wide and slope packway being paved with bricks leads to the city tower directly. The Pass city seemes deep and serene because of the semi-circular enclosure outside both east and west city gates as well as both frontispiece and city gate facing to different directions. The eastern semi-circular enclosure is called "Chaozong" and the western one the "Huiji". Another quadrate Pass majestically stands at 10-odd meters to the western semi-circular enclosure, at the side of the Pass city. The Pass city gate where vigorous Chinese words of " jiayuGuan" being inscribed, the only gate to pass in and out the jiayu Pass in ancient time. On the circumvallation, the eastern, middle and western towers stand majestically and opposite each other. Gazing into the distance from the Pass tower, sightseer will be excited by the panoramic view of the wonderful grandeur of the vast and desolate desert; the Great Wall, like a dragon, floats on the vast Gobi, rises and falls by turns; the view of it just as stated in the verse of "frontier's desert is immense, smoke of wolves' dung rises into sky, the setting sun makes it stand out." All these attract the sightseer's eyes, lingering about and forgetting to turn back. Jiayu Pass takes saw-toothed battlements on the tall and upright town wall where the unimaginable quantities of bricks used. As the story goes that these bricks were brought

Jiayu Pass, known as the Impregnable Pass in the world, is the starting point of the Great Wall in the Ming Dynasty.It has stood tall and upright at the western terminal of Gansu for more than 600 years. It is the western starting point of the Great Wall. With smart design and solid construction, the pass used to be a fortified military stronghold.

City tower on Jiayu Pass

from brick-kiln over 100li away by oxcarts, then being shouldered upstairs along steep packway by forced laborers. A wall built around the western circumvallation in company with the bounding walls standing in the east, south and north of the city. Both the south and north of the city, where the open wall situated in the south and concealed rampart in the north, connect with the Great Wall, and extend out along undulating low hills, as depicted in the verse of "Natural moat for national defence, and the impregnable pass in the world".

100-odd paces to the western gate of the Pass, a large stele stands with four powerful Chinese words of "Impregnable Pass in the World" being inscribed together with "Jiayu Pass Casual Notes", the poem with 44 line in total and five characters to a line written by XuYang-liang, the censor for Gan-Shan prefecture in the 44th year of Wanli in the Ming Dynasty (i.e.1616), being engraved on it, elegant in handwriting and fine in carving. The splendor and majesty of this Pass are vividly depicted. As the story goes that when the Jiayu Pass being built, YiZhan-kan, an old experienced craftsman who had "JiuJiu Arithmetic" at his fingers, worked out the number of bricks needed accurately and sworn he liked to be dealt with inexorably if his figure going awry, the supervising officer who took charge of the construction of the Pass did not believe him and crossly added a brick to the materials prepared. To their great surprise that only one brick left after the Pass had been accomplished and they were sincerely convinced. This brick, being called " Brick for Stabilizing City" and placed at a spot where it can be seen but not reached, is kept to commemorate this skillful craftsman. The every brick and wall there contains the countless wisdom, painstaking effort as well as the sweat of the ancient labouring people.

Crescent-shaped Spring

Dunhuang's Crescent-shaped Spring, being encircled with MingSha Mountain, distinguished for its crescent-shaped water body, is 30 m long from south to north and 20 m wide from east to west. Being deeper (about 5m in depth) in the east water and light in the west. The sky blue water looks like a sparkling and crystal-clear jade inlaid the sands; fascicular float grasses, flickering reeds and scattered willows grow around the spring body; the high-colored blue sky and desolate sands as well as water and shades set off mutually, all of them characterize the graceful Crescent-shaped Spring. As recorded in the Chinese ancient documents of "YuanHe prefectures and counties Annals"(YuanHe: the title of Emperor Li Chun's reign in Tang Dynasty, A.D.806~820) that "one spring water originating from MingSha Mountain and called "Sha Well", clear and sweat water lasts for centuries and never be covered with sands". Crescent-shaped Spring being call "Medical Spring" as well owing to the story that people will live forever and never grow old after eating "Tiebei Fish" and " Qixing Cao" within the spring water. As really depicted in "Dunhuang County Annals" that crescent-shaped water was blue, clear and bright as the mirror. It's a great geographical miracle that the spring water does never be dried up in the situation that the evaporation here being 100 times as large as the rainfall.

Crescent-shaped Spring, just as a very small basin between south and north mountains. Both protuberant north side of the southern mountain and recessed portion in the south side of the north mountain jointly result in the formation of the Crescent-shaped Spring. The wind direction will change into the easterly, souther as well as the Boreas after the northwest wind enters into the spring area, it moves centrifugally and the quicksand situated at the foot of the mountain would be carried to the top of it or opposite side of it. The wind's lift will force the slided sands to backtrack as long as the spring body's area hold the line. Both the quick sands and the spring water will naturally co-exist in a harmonious and contrary state. As stated in a poem of "Crescent-shaped Spring water being clear, blue and bright like a mirror; what matter if wind blows and sand beats, the inter-promoting relation exists between them, getting spring water to cook tea after strolling the spring". This poem written by a poet in the Qing Dynasty visually traced out the splendor of the Crescent-shaped Spring. 100-odd temple houses originally situated at the highland on the south bank of the spring. Pavilions, terraces and towers are close together in a row in serrate formation and setting off mutually. The scene is splendid, deep and serene. Such ancient architectures as Luzu Palace, Longshen Ancestral Temple, Damo Palace, Washou Palace,

Crescent Moon Spring

Grescent Moon Spring

Mingsha College, Crescent-shaped Spring Hall as well as Thor Dias add much lustre to the mystic Crescent-shaped Spring. Starting from the 4th year of QingYong-zheng's reign (i.e.1726), the Qing's local government, after the large quantities of people being internally migrated to Shazhou, went in for large-scale construction at the ruin of original Crescent-shaped Spring of the Song and Yuan Dynasties. As a result of it, the Crescent-shaped Spring became the important Taoist site where large quantities of adherents were attracted in Dunhuang region. This situation can be traced back to the 6-Dynasties or far ahead of them.

During the years from the 6-Dynasties to the both Tang and Song Dynasties, both the Buddhism and Taoism prevailed in Dunhuang region best. Mogao was known as the Holy Land of Buddhism and the Crescent-shaped Spring for Taoist in Dunhuang region. Unfortunately few people know the later, luckily, "Shazhou Annlas", the document with the serial number of S•788 and unearthed at Sutras-Stored Grotto tells it. As recorded in it that "Sha Well"(i.e. Crescent -shaped Spring) was deficient in "Toulong", alias "placing golden dragon model, jade and Taoist magic figures or incantations" or "sending golden dragon model and Taoist magic figures or incantations". The above mentioned are recorded in the "Shang Qing Ling Bao Da Fa", "Ling Bao Yu Jian", "Ling Bao Ling Jiao Ji JingShu", DuGuang -ting's "Tai Shang Huang Lu Zhai Yi" as well as "ceremony of sending golden dragon model, jade and Taoist magic figures or incantations" No.P•2354 Dunhuang document . "Toulong", for purpose of praying for blessings, happiness, well-being, or prosperity, was carried out as follows: placing or sending golden dragon model, jade and Taoist magic figures or incantation at mountains, in the ground or into the water. The religious ceremony of "Toulong", from the Northern Wei to Northern Song Dynasties, especially in both Tang and Song Dynasties, prevailed in Dunhuang and any other regions. As for the well-known mountains, most of them pertain to Buddhist. The Dunhuang's Buddhist temple gives priority to Mogao grotto, and Taoism, known as the traditional Chinese culture, takes Mingsha Mountains and Crescent-shaped Spring as its beachhead together with the nearby Taoist temple as the sacrificial altar.

The limpid Crescent-shaped Spring, looking up the sky as it were a bright eye, and being accompanied by loaches, "Tiebei" fish as well as "QixinCao" in seed, is encircled with Mingsha Mountain. The sand does not wreak havoc on it though millions upon millions of years being past, the mountain becomes mysterious for the accompanying spring there and the fantastic spring because of the mountains around. Two of them set off mutually, and make their oddity and splendor stand out.

Mingsha Mountain

Towering and grand Mingsha Mountain, being known for its thundering sound made by quick sands, accumbently lies in the desert 5 km to the north of the town four several thousands of years and undulatingly stretches out as it were a dragon by overlooking south from Dunhuang county. It, starting from Mogao Grotto and ending at Dangxiang River, is 40 km from east to west and 20km from south to north. Mingsha Mountain made of the accumulated sands being consisted of red, yellow, green, white as well as black silver sands, as the name implies, it's called "wusesha". Mingsha Mountain looks bright under sunlight, its beauty and grandeur stands far ahead of that of the general mountains. The quicksand will make thundering sound as long as People slide down along mountainside. To people's surprise that the slid sands will return back owing to the unique lift of the wind at night there. No any changes happened to Mingsha Mountain though hundreds of years past. As a result of it, Mingsha Mountain becomes into one of eight beauty spots.

Early in the latter period of the Eastern Han Dynasty(i.e. A.D.200), records related to Mingsha Mountain could be found in "XinShi central Shanxi plain Record"that "shajiao mountain, existing in Hexi region, is more arduous than stone mountains are. The yellow coarse sand would give away and make a loud sound just as drumbeat and clarino producing while people climb it". The pioneer records related to this rustle sound can go far back to " Western Lands Atlas" and " Tang's Western Lands Records" though it's not exclusive. As recorded in Vol.40 "YuanHe prefectures and counties annals"(YuanHe: the title of Emperor Li Chun's reign in Tang Dynasty, A.D.806~820)" that "being the sandy mountain with arduous ridges and peaks", " loud sound being made as long as people climbing it"; another records in "Old Tang's Annals" said that " residents within the town can hear the rustle sound made by the sandy mountain in unclouded days". As stated in history record that early before 1000 years ago, our ancestry took the convention of sliding mountain, especially in "dragon boat festival" in both the Tang and Song Dynasties. As to the origin of Mingsha Mountain, people can refer to "YiYuan", the book written by LiuJing-shu, the Huangmen Lang (an official title under the monarchy in ancient china) in early times of the Southern and Northern Dynasties. In the middle-period of the 5th century, as story goes that Mingsha Mountain coming of accumulated skeletons of being defeated in the war which were covered with sands lately, as a result of it, the drumbeat and clarino could often be heard. The fact that Mingsha Mountain has existed for 1000-odd years is indubitable although above legend prevails. Mingsha Mountain has become into amusement ground. As recorded in "Dunhuang Record", No. S•5448 document, that "all young men and women, in "dragon boat festival", assembling on the Mingsha Mountaintop and then sliding down together, and the thundering sound, thereout, being made". No body knows the reason of Mingsha Mountain making a thundering sound till now. As explained in"Origin and Secret of Mingsha Mountain and Sound-Making" written by ZhangWei-guo, CAS Desert Research Institute, that rustle caused by the following reasons: ① the sound comes from sliding sands whose interspaces change differently so that the air would go in and out ever and agah, as a result of it, the sound is made;②the resonance produces while the seismic wave of dried sand being transmitted to the layer of sand soil under the sand dune;③ the exterior of sandy mountain is very dry and rich in quartz, the sands rub each other to make a sound while wind blowing and people going round on them in the sun; ④ The quartz is sensitive to the pressure, the static electricity occurs while being continuously extruded, and conversely it telescopically convulses, the static interaction ,thereout, results in making a sound.

Mingsha Mountain in Gansu

Bright Pearl on the Gobi Desert, South Lake in Dunhuang

Dunhuang's Wowa Pool

Dunhuang's Wowa Pool, alias "ShouChang Hai" or "ShouChang Ze" for the ancient Guchang Town nearby, is situated at 70km to the southwest of Dunhuang city, 4km to the seat of Nanhu Village Office. It's called "Huangba Reservoir", the storage pool made of numerous spring water Nowadays. The purl of running water, adumbral trees as well as the boundless greenbelt and grassplot together characterize it, the perfect natural pasture as well as the suitable wasteland to open up and grow food grain from of old. People, placing themselves in it, would let themselves forget the Gobi desert around them and seem entering into watery region in south China, with the result that it's called "Sai Shang Jiang Nan".

Here to be said the old sod of legendary "heavenly steed". As recorded in "Shouchang County Landforms", the Dunhuang document, that "ShouChang Hai" situated at 10li to the south of Shouchang county town, being one li in circumference and fathomless where BaiLi-chang captured the "heavenly steed"., As recorded in "Hanshu· Emperor Wu Record" that "in June of the 4th year of Yuanding, a tripod caldron being found near the earth god temple, in autumn, a "heavenly steed" appeared in Wowa Pool, a tripod caldron and a chaunt being cast and written respectively for it". This story happed as follows: in the 3rd year of Yuanshou of the Emperor Wu's reign (i.e.120 B.C), BaiLi-chang, a courtling and being exiled to graze horses nearby Wowa Pool, one day, a larruping one among groups of wild horses which regularly came to drink waters came into his eyes. The small and square-built horse's head, big and bright eyes, small ears and big nose, gentle underlip and steep and square-built muffle, powerful and square-backed horseback, wide and patulous thorax, round knee as well as thin and long legs and fast speed together characterize it. BaiLi-chang firstly placed a dummy made of reed at the place where wild horses drank water regularly, as time passes, they accustomed to it. BaiLi-chang stood there in place of it and succeeded in lassoing the horse. He fabricated that this horse was the heavenly horse sprung from Wowa Pool in order to atone for his crime, the emperor Wu, who was fond of horses, was excited by it and thought it was the heavenly steed granted by his most respectful TaiYi God (i.e. Polaris), he named it the "TaiYi Tima" and wrote him a chaunt. It said that TaiYi God conferred this heavenly steed on him, whose sweat and saliva perspired were red and odoriferous while running, it could walk ten thousand miles within a day if being out of restriction, only the dragon flown in the sky can become his qualified friend. People, standing on the bank of Huangba Reservoir, having this legendary called to mind and pondered, overlooking the boundless meadow and lake water nearby, forget to turn back. In 1983, the construction in full scale was carried out to reinforce the slope protection of Huangba Reservoir where $200m^3$ water being hold in company with 130-odd fish being put every year, as a result of it, it becomes a natural fish pond, green and bright pearl in the desert as well as an important aquatic amusement among beauty plots in Dunhuang city.

Beacon Tower at the Yangguan Pass Scenic Spot in Dunhuang

Yangguan Pass

Yangguan Pass, being situated with the boundary of Nanhu village, 70km to the southwest of Dunhuang proper, lies to the south of Longtou Mountain (i.e. Dundun Mountain nowadays), with the result that it's called Yangguan Pass according to Chinese traditional statement of south of a hill or north of a river to be "Yang". The original Pass town will never be seen nowadays with exception of remnant beacon tower, being 4. 7m tall, 8～7.5m long and wide for its bottom and 8～6.8m long and wide for its roof top, being left in actual existence on Dundun Mountain. Sightseer will have a view of all in the circumference of tens of meters while standing on the beacon tower. As a result of it, it's called the "eyes and ears of Yangguan Pass".

No ancient Yangguan Pass town can be found nowadays. As for its original location, there are different versions of the story. As stated in "Kuodi Record", "Yuanhe Annals" as well as "Huanyu Records" that Yangguan Pass lying at 6 li to the west of Shouchang county in shazhou; in "Xin Tang Shu (New History of the Tang Dynasty) • geography" that " another route going to the old town of the Yangguan Pass from the place at 10li to the west of Shouchang county in shazhou". As recorded in the hand-copied "Shazhou Atlas" stored in Paris that Yangguan Pass "lying at 10 li to the west of county and only remains of it being kept in actual existence". As a result of it, the definite location of original Yangguan Pass should be at 10 li to the west of the ancient Shouchang county, namely the "GudongTan (curios beach)" because of the river, small basin and remains of ancient enceinte, etc. there. The natural conditions there are suitable for living. The nowaday Yangguan Pass may be a large beacon tower nearby the original real one because of no signs indicating that it had ever been an impregnable pass in ancient time. Yangguan Pass, being under the jurisdiction of Yangguan Douwei(title of the military officer subter general) in the Han Dynasty, was an important frontier pass as well as the only way for southern route of the Silk-road to pass through. The Yangguan county ever being set up by Jin Dynasty was abolished after the Tang Dynasty. No name of "GudongTan (curios beach)", being situated in the west of the farmlands, north of Yuantaizi Mountain, east of Qingshanzi Ridge as well as south of Dundun Mountain, could be found from historical records. The boundless quick sands stretch to the horizon. 20-odd arrays of inartificial sandbanks are being formed from south to north naturally. Some grit and flats together with relics of ancient weapons, currencies, tools of production, living articles, adornments and relics of wares, etc. exist in sandy trenches. The remains of houses, kilns, cob walls, farmlands and trenches also

Beacon Tower at the Yangguan Pass Scenic Spot in Dunhuang

being found there. The name of "GudongTan (curios beach) " comes of the plenty of sites of ancient people and exposed cultural relics there. It's the site of the Han's Yangguan Pass or the seat of Yangguan county after the Han Dynasty considered by the historian. The clear and orderly arranged foundations as well as wall base with intermittently width and area of over $10000m^2$ nearby the Yangguan Pass represent the prosperity of it in former days. Xuanzhuang, known as the hierarch in the Tang Dynasty, entered into Yangguan Pass after coming back from India with sutras. Yangguan Pass, nowadays, becomes the pronoun of original desolate frontier pass. Frequent wars, excessive reclamation and cultivation in history deteriorated the vegetation, water source and the entironment there. With the result that residents here gradually migrated to other places after the times of the Song and Liao Dynasties. The original prosperity of both Yangguan Pass and ancient Shouchang town had been covered with hardhearted and rolling qicksands after the Yuan Dynasty. In the poem of "Yangguan Sandie (i.e. refrain reiterative sentence)" written by WangWei, the great poet in the Tang Dynasty, he wrote that "in Weicheng(i.e.Xianyang city nowadays), the morning's shower stoped as soo as it just moistened the dust on road, guest houses together with trees along the road shew their colors; my friend, please drinking more! No old friends could accompany you as long as you going west of Yangguan Pass." This poem handed down for centuries arouses people's curiosities related to the original prosperous Yangguan Pass.

Yumen Pass

Yumen Pass

Yumen Pass, alias "XiaoFangpancheng", and "DielieBanjin" in Mongolian, lies about 90km to the northwest of Dunhuang county, known as the only way for both Western Lands's and Hetian's jades coming from Tarim Basin to be transported to the central plains, was under the jurisdiction of Yumen Pass Douwei (title of the military officer subter general) in the Western Han Dynasty and ever being closed together with the Silk-road before long after WangMang had seized the sceptre. The Silk-road was recovery after Banchao being sent to take charge of the Western Lands, unfortunately, during 100-odd years from the Jianwu to Yanguang of the Eastern Han's regime, this Silk-road between the east and west had experienced three times of obstruction and recovery. Yumen Pass, in the Eastern Han Dynasty, was under the domination of Yumen Zhangwei. The Silk-road has declined since the Two Jin and Southern and Northern Dynasties owing to the frequent wars and developed ocean shipping between the east and west afterwards,

The first rays of the morning sun at the Yumen Pass

especially in both Sui and Tang Dynasties, the YiWu thoroughfare to the Western Lands was clear and the Yumen Pass was moved to Jinchang county in Guazhou (i.e.place nearby the Shuangtabao within Anxi county nowadays). Such original prosperity as to-and-fro trade caravans and envoys not existed any more with exception of desolate and vast Gobi desert and sands. As a result of it, WangZhi-huan signed out in his poem of "Liangzhou Ci": "the chopping and riband-shaped Yellow River runs mountains high, borders on clouds in the distance, how lonely both desolate town and towering mountains are ! Don't complain no green sallows for friends because of the spring breeze being far from Yumen Pass."

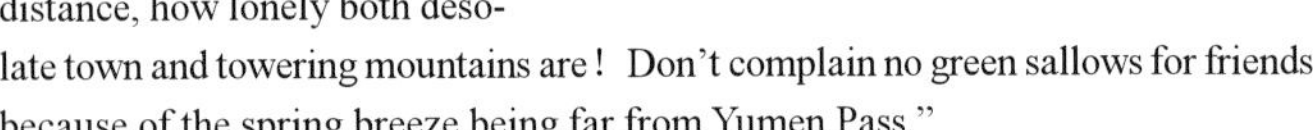

The ancient "XiaoFangpancheng" town, being called Yumen Pass nowadays, is square-shaped with bounding clay wall being reserved perfectly. The gates on western and northern walls become distortion just as a hole because of the flake of walls and the lower part of northern gate is obstructed. The town wall of ancient "XiaoFangpancheng" town, with remnant area of over 600m², is 24.5m long from east to west, 26.4m wide from south to north and 9.7m in remnant height; 3.7m in upper width, 4m in lower width of eastern wall and 4.9m in lower width of northern wall. A 1.3m wide walkway goes around circumvallation top, 85 cm thick for the inner parapet wall and 1.5m for outer one. A 83cm wide packway situated at southeast corner within the town goes south along the southern wall and reaches the top where the harmonious view constituted by Mazong Mountain, blue and clear Hala Lake as well as the sandbanks, Gobi desert and site of the Great Wall can be overlooked. No one believes here had ever been an ancient battlefield "being densely covered with war clouds, and littered with corpses". Looking southwest, the sites of ancient beacon towers intermittently extend through to Luobubo within Xinjiang autonomous region.

Yadan Landform

Yadan Landform, alias "demoniac town", lies 180 km to the northwest of the Dunhuang city proper. The broad, flat-topped elevation with one or more cliff-like sides and several or scores of meters tall, common in Gobi desert in northwest China together characterize it. It's called "wind-erosion mesa" with "Yadan Landform" as its scientific name.

The word of "Yadan" means "cliff", the inflexion of "Yaerdan". ChenJia-qi, the Chinese famous geographer who ever went into the Luobubo area twice at the early days of the last century and called the group of "wind-erosion mesas" the "Yadan", the universal term of the geography afterwards. The causes of formation of them are many and varied because the ocean existed west of Luobubo area (with Dunhuang region included). Lakes and swamp countries formed along with the upthrust, then the Gobi desert emerged after the lakes had been dried up. As for these mesas, their unique landforms came from the old seabed corroded in glacier times. The Paleozoic fossils, for example the 1997's fossil of ancient elephant, are unearthed at mesas within Luobubo area.

The distance of loess-colored Yadan landforms measures 25km from east to west, and about 5km wide from south to north as well as over10m higher than the floor is. Towers, pavilions as well as the birds and beasts of various shapes can come into view while looking into the distance. There are entitled imaginable and fair-sounding names of "general's service cap", "cock heralding the break of a day", "opening fire with artillery", "hell's gate", "finding the moon from the seabed", "fleet going into battle", "bear forest", " peacock princess", "Pisa leaning tower", "sit in meditation" and "lion roaring", etc. Extraordinary rocks, serried and perilous peak ever change and result in the thoughts flashing across one's mind, just as a vast floating aerodrome floated on the boundless sea freely. The ancient Silk-road is in the north of these Yadan landforms and Kumutage Desert in the south of it. Wandering through the "high streets and back lanes" in this "castle", the demoniac sound caused by the movement of both wind and airflow can be heard ghastfully. The name of "demoniac town" just comes of it. The people look negligible while wandering into this community created by the nature where no flower, grass and bird can be seen. The scores of wide gaps formed naturally in this landform of over 100km^2 in area face both south and north just as thoroughfares. The various Yadan landforms on both sides look like the "residential areas" of various architectural shapes in big cities. They can't be matched for placidity. The tall and big Yadan mesas stand same as rows of towering buildings. It's not only like an ancient great large city but also a huge and mysterious labyrinth. This multicolored art world is the masterpiece produced by the sand blown by wind in desert and is extraordinary as if done by the spirits. Its grandeur and spectacularity could never be matched by any other artworks.

The Mystical Yadan Landforms in Dunhuang

The Mystical Yadan Landforms in Dunhuang

The Han's Great Wall in Dunhuang

The Emperor Wu, after the Jiuquan Prefecture had been set up in A.D121, ordered to build "Ting (small mound)", " Zhang(large mound)" as well as "Se(the Great Wall)" west of Lingju(i.e. Yongdeng), station beacon troops and open up wasteland there concurrently led by Houguan and Houzhang (i.e. military officer). Within the years of Yuanfeng of the emperor HanWu-di's reign(i.e.A. D.110～105), the Han government started to build frontier fortress west of Jiuquan. "Ting(small mound)", " Zhang(large mound)" and "Se(the Great Wall)" extended through to Yumen. As recorded in " Hanshu·Chongguo Biography" that "measuring 11,500 miles from Dunhuang to Liaodong, thousands of soldiers garrisoned there" as well as in " Hanshu·Western Lands Biography" that "the Western Lands was horror-struck and sent envoys to pay tributes to the Han Dynasty one after another, conversely, Han's envoys to the Western Lands were appointed the posts there after ErShi, the general, led armed forces to suppress DaWan State, as a result of it, Tings(small mound)" were built along the way from Jiuquan and Dunhuang to Yanze.

The Great Wall between Dunhuang and Luobubo had been accomplished within the years of Taichu. At present time, the sites of Han's Great Wall, extending over100li and starting from Anxi's Dongjiandun in the east, going to north along the south bank of Shule River windingly, then winding their way to west and ending at Yanze right in the west, can be found in the Gobi desert in Northwest China. It shows that Han government highly valued Jiuquan, and symbolizes the resolute sprit of the Chinese Nation.

The most sections of Han's Great Wall passed through reedy marshlands. As a result of that, the Great Wall was made of layer upon layer of mud, sand and reed, and then being tamped. The large section of Han's Great Wall, especially 10-odd km outside of Yumen Pass is well kept in actual existence owing to the saline-alkali mucus in mud and sand. This remnant wall was made of loess and auxiliaries of reeds, Chinese tamarisk, diversiform-leaveed parlor as well as Luobuma, etc. It's 4m tall, 5cm in thickness of the auxiliary, 20cm in that of sandy soil layer and clear in tamped soil layer. They are matted together hard. The 10m tall remnant mounds of beacon tower built by laying adobes in company with spare firewood in stork in those days can be seen there. The crotch of one section of the Great Wall which going west along Jingta county, Qiaowan, Anxi and ending at Yumen Pass (i.e."XiaoFangpancheng" lies about 90km to the northwest of Dunhuang county) in succession is at Shangxia Jiadunwan in Jingta county where one branch goes southwest along Daciwan and links with the eastern part of the Eastern Han's Great Wall within Gaotai County; another one goes north and reaches Juyan Town (i.e. area east of Ejinaqi and west of Jinsutu Lake nowadays). The section of Great Wall between Jiuquan and Dunhuang was built in the 3rd year of Yuanfeng (i.e. A. D.108) after ZhaoPo-nu captured the Hun tribe who occupied the region west of Ruoshui and north of Mazong Mountain in both prefectures of Jiuquan and Dunhuang of that time and usually entered into Hexi region along Ruoshui valley after climbing over Mazong Mountain or got to Juyanhai.

Beacon Tower

The castle was built together with the beach tower or beach bound inside the Great Wall at a distance from each other. The beach tower was called "Ting (small mound)" or "Sui(large mound)" with certain number of beacon troops led by Houzhang or Suizhang(military officer). The large castle and beach tower called "Zhang" were built in several castles interval with large number of beacon troops stationed there led by Houguan.

The Han's tower-shaped beacon towers mainly were built inside the Great Wall with exception of the few outside. Their four different structures are as follows: ① being built and tamped by laying loessial puddle; ② being built by laying natural harden soil, stone, braches of Chinese tamarisk and diversiform-leaved poplar, they were 20～30cm in every thickness, then spreading a layer of reeds on each of them; ③ being built by laying stones, and covering it with a layer of reeds between two tiers of stones; ④ being built by laying adobes being made of loess and sandstone mixed with short reedy stems. The adobe was 40cm in length, 20cm in width and about 14cm in thickness. To cover with a layer of thin reeds in several 3～5 tiers of soil interval. As for some beach towers, they were built by laying sandstone and reedy stems completely. With respect to the space between Han's beacon towers, some are within a kilometer, some are tens of kilometers apart though the statement of being 5 li apart between two small beacon towers and 10 li apart between two large ones recorded in history. The most beacon towers were built at highlands so as to oversee and inform enemy's situation at once because of convenient signal fire situation. The height of every beacon tower based upon the topography where being built. For example, only 2 m in height for beacon towers built on mesas in the Yadan landforms, by contraries, the above 7m in height for those built in the Gobi desert. The beacon towers built nearby Dunhuang's Xihu, being about 10m in remnant height and7～8m in length of every bottom hemline, are still preserved completely owing to dry climate conditions there. The parapet walls around the top of the beacon tower formed a small room.

The function of beacon tower is to oversee, inform the enemy's situation and give an alarm at once by the aid of the smoke given by wolves' dung in daytime and firebrand at night. Faggoted reeds (called "torch"), Chinese tamarisk and diversiform-leaved poplar (called "firewood") were major materials piled up nearby the beacon tower. Some beacon towers in company with the rest "firewood", more than 15 piles nearby many beacon towers, of those days can be seen in Dunhuang owing to being richly endowed by nature there. These ancient messengers, the eyewitness of the history, had ever won great honor and distinction in special time of the history though being laid off at present time and standing there desolately.

Beacon Tower by the Great Wall

White Horse Pagoda in Dunhuang

White Horse Pagoda

The White Horse Pagoda lies to the south of ancient Dunhuang's town, 2km to the center of Dunhuang city. Novel-shaped, simple and exquisite, 9 levels in total as well as 12m in height and 7m in diameter characterize it. As for its structure, it's built by laying adobes and vertical shaft coated with the mixture of grass and mud as well as lime, eight-square-shaped ground floor covered by laying long and narrow bricks, 3m in length of every bottom hemline. Folding corners and clinker-built structure are employed for the construction of the 2nd to 4th floors. Ball-shaped nails are around the lower surface and the petals of upward lotus on upside of the 5th floor respectively. Overturned bowl-shaped structure is employed by the 6th floor and wheel-shaped form by the 7th floor as well as a hexagonal Pocha Plate on the top of the pagoda in company with big wind-bells hung on every corner.

The pagodas, being ancient building, rise into the clouds and can be seen everywhere in China. It's called "Baota"(tower) because of being exquisitely made and ever decorated with such seven treasures as gold, silver, glazed tiles as well as agates and bronze bells by Buddhist monks. The pagoda came of India, being called "STUPA" in Sanskrit and "Sudubo", "Tapo" and "Futu", etc in Chinese. The pagoda was initially built for the relics of Buddha (Sakyamuni). The common pagodas in large variety are as follows: round, quadrate, hexagonal, octagonal and dodecagonal in shape; cores of meters as well as very one inch in height; wood, adobe, stone, brick and metal, etc. in structure. The pagoda, with the advance of religion, becomes the building in memory of Buddhist masters and animals made greater contribution to the Buddhism. The pagodas built for Buddhist masters can be found everywhere, the other way round, those built for animals are few. Dunhuang's White Horse Pagoda was built for Kumarajiva's horse being sick to death, as a result of that, the special historical significance thus can be seen.

The legend goes that in the year of 384, Kumarajiva, the great translator of sutras in Qiuci State, rode a white horse named "Tianliu" eastwards Changan to carry forward the Buddhist doctrine. "Tianliu", Kumarajiva 's right hand, scaled mountains and forded streams as well as knew ways and water source. Unfortunately, the horse caught a disease in Dunhuang and ate nothing for days, Kumarajiva, had his face covered with scowl and lost his appetite because of very long way left for him. One night, the horse appeared in his dream and made a request that he was "Tianliu", one of heavenly steeds, received the order to send Kumarajiva to propagate Buddhism eastwards because of difficulty journeys prior to entering into the frontier juncture, now, the mission was fulfilled and he could not accompany Kumarajiva any longer, Dunhuang would be his destination and niavana. His long-cherished wish had already become a fact, too. Kumarajiva held the horsetail, followed after it and flagitated that propagating Buddhism being great event, should not give up halfway and suffer defeat on the verge of victory. The horse told Kumarajiva that was the providence and another heavenly steed was waiting for him in nearby Hulu valley while Kumarajiva crying his heart out and being reluctant to part with. Even now, Kumarajiva still held horsetail and to be loath to part. Suddenly, Kumarajiva 's dream was interrupted by the neigh, he waked up and being told the death of his white horse. He was so grieved that he built this pagoda for the horse at large expenses. The 9-levels pagoda shows horse being at 9 years of age. Both varied shapes and decorative patterns such as lotus petals, eight-square-shaped ground floor, etc on every level are rite or religious ceremony for the white horse so that it could go to the Elysium by stepping on the lotus. The legend says that on July 24 of every lunar year, people can hear the neigh of the white horse under the White Horse Pagoda where the horse was buried on July 24.

The appearance of the Mogao Grotto

Mogao Grotto

Mogao Grotto, alias "Thousand Buddha Grotto" popularly, lies on the cliff west of Dangquan River between Sangwei Hills and Mingsha Mountain, 25km to the southeast of Dunhuang county. The earliest records related to establishing Mogao Grotto written by Tang's personnel can be found from "Boxi" and No.3720 Vol. of Dunhuang literature. As recorded in it that "a Buddhist monk, with monk's cane, once walked alone through Sanwei and Minsha Mountains, he look up by accident and found countless golden Buddha rushing out of rays of sunshine just on the top of Minsha Mountain wonderfully, and was moved deeply. He thought that Minsha Mountain the specific spot for Buddhism and this just the lot by which he was brought to see the omniscient Buddha with his own eyes, and he was suggested intentionally to carry forward the power of Buddha here. He vowed and excavated the first grotto in the piedmont east of the Minsha hill. Then, FaLiang, another Buddhist monk from the east, excavated the second grotto beside the first one owing to the magical providence happened to him there. Both of them were the founder of the temple there. SikongSuo-jing in the Jin Dynasty named it the "Xiankong Temple". More than 500 grottoes were excavated successively there since that time. In the 2nd year of Yanzai, the Buddhist monk LingYin together with lay Buddhist YinZu established the northern huge Buddha figure 140 chi tall; in the year of Kaiyuan, Buddhist monk ChuYan in company with his fellow villager MaSi-zhong established the southern huge Buddha figure 120 chi tall; the Buddhist monk Shan Xi built the hall in the year of Kaihuang. 490 years had past since the first grotto was excavated in the 3rd year of Dali. There were 496 years as of the year of Tang's Gengwu. These records were written on fifteenth of the first month of the lunar year (the 6th year of Xiantong in TangDynasty). It's noticeable that the 3rd year of Dali in this document referred to the year of 768. The year before 404years just was the 6th year of Ganlu (before the 1st year of Jianyuan) of the Early Qin Dynasty (i.e.364), also called the 2nd year of Xingning of the Emperor An's reign of the Eastern Jin Dynasty. They are bases for calculating the correct time related to the establishment of Mogao Grotto. As for 496 years, if it's right, the "Gengwu" should be "Gengchen (i.e.the year of 860, the 1st year of Xiantong)" instead, there are just 496 years in total from the year of 364 to 860. As recorded in cliff records that over 500 grottoes had been excavated in Mogao Grotto before the Early Tang Dynasty, but only 492 serial numbers can be seen at the present time owing to the terrible havoc caused by an earthquake taken there there at the beginning of the Tang Dynasty. Many remnant murals there of the Sui Dynasty explained this statement. The part of 492existent grottoes were repaired and re-excavated after that earthquake.

Someone says that what recorded in the cliff records only referred to the niche. With respect to grottoes there, someone of them coexisted with two, three or four niches, as a result, the statement of over 500

Big Arch

Mogao Grotto among trees

grottoes or niches there is reasonable, too.

Being situated at inland and encircled with Gobi desert, typical continental climate, strong solar radiation, rich sunshine as well as little rainfall and high evaporation characterize Dunhuang. Mogao Grotto lies on an oasis less than 1km^2 in circumference where the Dangquan River flows for centuries and provides for lives and artistic treasury there. Total 492 grottoes of the 16-States Period, Northern Wei, Western Wei, Northern Zhou and the Sui, Tang, Five, Song and Yuan Dynasties and the Western Xia Regime, together with 45000-odd m^2 murals as well as 2400 painted sculptures and 5 wooden buildings of both the Tang and Song Dynasties are kept in actual existence although they experiencing the long-term destruction of both nature and mankind. It's the most integrated, largest and existent Buddhist artistic treasury in the world, and one of the World Cultural Heritages protected by UN.

The illustrational murals are important part of Mogao Grotto art being called the "mural art corridor" 1m tall and 45km long if all illustrational murals being arranged. This "mural art corridor" employs 32 kinds of illustrations of the sutras as follows: 2 illustrations of "Futian" sutra, 70 illustrations of Lotus sutra, 97 illustrations of Maitreya sutra, 71 illustrations of Amita sutra, 84 illustrations of Sukhavativyuha sutra, 76 illustrations of the Pure Land sutra, 111 illustrations of Bhaisajya sutra, 11 illustrations of nirvana sutra, 1 illustration of "Baoyu" sutra, 29 illustrations of Hua-yen sutra, 10 illustrations of Golden-light sutra, 17 illustrations of diamond sutra, 11 illustrations of Lanka sutra, 31 illustrations of "Tianqingwen" sutra, 12 illustrations of "Siyi-Brahma asking" sutra, 5 illustrations of "Xianyu" sutra, 32 illustrations of requite favours sutra, 4 illustrations of repaying parent obligation sutra, 3 illustrations of Braham sutra, 4 illustrations of "Miyan" sutra, 2 illustrations related to being in meditation as universal wise sovereign wining Tuoluoni sutra. Many illustrations of thousand Buddha, 18 illustrations of "Raudraksa's battle" sutra, 66 illustrations of Vimallakivti sutra, 17 illustrations of Kwan-yin sutra, 132 illustrations of Manjusri sutra, 125 illustrations of Samantabhadra sutra, 15 illustrations of Ti-tsang's 10 kings sutra, 40 illustrations of the thousand-hand and eye Manjunatha Kwan-yin sutra, 57 illustrations of Amoga Kwan-yin sutra, 65 illustrations of Talismanic-wheel Kwan-yin sutra and 16 illustrations of thousand-hand Manjusri sutra holding thousand bowls in hands. The every illustration's style as well as Bodhisattva's appearance differs, for example, graceful and charming flying devi, kindly Bodhisattva, Buddha's powerful and bold warrior attendants, double-dealing heathens and ever changing color edgings, etc. They enrich this artistic hall. These illustrative stories of different dynasties not only bear incomparable artistic values but also reflect the social reality of those days directly or indirectly, for instance the working scene of farmers and the dominator's life of wanton extravagance, grand ancient building, means of communication of the Silk-road, the ancient habits and customs of wedding and funeral. What the murals reflected can be based on while researching the life in ancient society.

The murals related to both Buddhist historical sites and donors are also the indispensability of Dunhuang mural. The murals of Buddhist historical site represent the feature of Chino-Buddhism where many picturesque Buddhist historical materials being kept. The contents of 67 murals in 40 Buddhist historical sites relate to the following: Buddhist history story; Grateful and thankful story; Buddhist master's story; stone images as well as Buddhist topography and miracles. They delineate Buddhist historical characters, events, miracles and other relevant stories rooted in historical materials and folk legends. They could be referred to while studying Buddhist development history.

3000-odd donor figures, their figures and names were inscribed in caves in appreciation of their donations to the excavation of the grottoes, are kept in actual existence. As for the size of donor figures there, the earliest donor's figure is smallest, even about

Cishi (Maitreya) Tower

one inch in size. The size of the latest donor's figure is about as large as life. The donors' identities are diversified as follows: magistrates, officers and soldiers garrisoned the frontier, monasteries, common people, servants and minority characters. Their figures were arranged together with their servants in accordance with strict ranking system of master's figures standing in the front rank in large size and the servant's figure at the rear in small size. Some master's figures are accompanied by hundreds upon hundreds servant's figures, some has few. The Tang's donor figures were at the height of splendor. Being true to life, lively personality, vivid manner and magnificence characterize them together and to be the real portraiture of the society of those days. What being inscribed there were actual persons and events, but few of them could be found in relevant historical materials. They are rare indispensability to research the history related to politic, military affair, religion, nationality as well as the cultural exchange between the east and west happened to Dunhuang, Hexi and the Silk-road.

Too many florid murals to see as well as varied and painted sculpture art being true to life. The 492 grottoes are decorated with 2400-odd painted sculptures tri-dimensionally and visually. Kindly Buddha, Bodhisattva showing pleasant smiles, Buddha's powerful and bold warrior attendants of as tall as 30-odd m or as small as about one inch in size, sightseers seem to be placed in the Buddha's world. Dunhuang art as well as the painted sculpture art was at the height of splendor in the Tang Dynasty. The contemplative and smiled Bodhisattva's painted sculptures in Cave 325, Cave 35 and Cave 45, etc. are just as pretty lady exposed her neck and shoulders, dressed in soft and transparent shirred silk next to the skin; by contraries, those of Maharajas, Buddha's warrior attendants and Narayana look powerful, bold, strong and handsome; Sakyamuni's sagacity and worldly wise; Kasyapa's tact and run deep as well as Anada's puerility and honesty, etc. Their sensibility and expressions were vividly depicted. The layout of painted sculptures in grottoes are as follows: Sakyamuni's figure was centered in niche and be accompanied by Kuan-yin and Mahasthamaprapta's figures on both sides and Kasyapa's and Anada's standing on two sides of the niche (many of them are statues or paintings) under the guardianship of the figures of Buddha's warrior attendants outside the niche. These painted sculptures, in which the painter's sensibility being agglomerated, surge people's soul. The excavation of Hunan's "Mawangdui", the exposure of Ming's and Qing's archives, the coming up out of land of Juyan's bamboo slips of the Han Dynasty as well as the finding of the Sutras-Stored Grotto in Dunhuang are regarded as the four great achievements for cultural and artistic archaeology in modern times. The Cave 17 is called Sutras-Stored Grotto particularly where all visitors try to be the first to see it. As the story goes that one day in 1900, a Taoist WangYuan-lu found it while cleaning out the piled sands in this grotto measured 2.7m from east to west, and 2.8mi from south to north as well as 2.5m in height with over 50,000 volumes of scriptures and documents together with tapestry portraits, musical instruments used in a Buddhist mass and countless cultural relics related to about ten Dynasties from the 4th to 11th centuries in it. They come down to the politics, economy, military affairs, history, philosophy, religion, nationalities and literature, etc. of over 1000 years in ancient China. They are to be rich and valuable materials for researching Chinese ancient history and result in the emergence of "Dunhuang Study" in the world. They play more and more important role in promoting the academic exchange on Dunhuang studies between China and other countries all over the world.

Bodhisattva, Cave 194, the High Tang Dynasty

Cross-legged Maitreya, Cave 275, the Northern Liang Dynasty

Cross-legged Maitreya in Cave 275

As to the question of who is the host of this Cave, Bodhisattva, Maitreya, or Sakyamuni? No specific conclusion can be referred to. Generally speaking, that Bodhisattva is not permitted to stay at the master's position. Comparing with such eighty features as head sculpture and appearance, the features of it do not pertain to myriad characteristics of Buddha. Maitreya and Buddha share the same symbols according to sutras as follows: wearing the crown, chaplet, jade-like stones, petticoat and sleeveless outer garment that hangs from the shoulders, exposing his neck and barefoot, sitting up and being cross-legged, people pursuantly called it Cross-legged Maitreya for the moment.

Cross-legged Maitreya's statue, one of magnum opuses in Mogao grotto, being molded in Cave275 in the time of the Northern Liang's regime, centered in the niche on the wall faced the south. Wearing samadhi crown and jade-like stones and sheepskin and pleated petticoat, long hairs hanging down loosely and orderly, exposing his neck, as well as sleeveless outer garment that hangs from the shoulders; triangular backrest, sitting up on the double lions seat and being cross-legged; no coiled bun except for a shock of black hairs, plump and longish visage, Roman nose, fine brows and protrusive eyes, wide shoulder and plain breast, stocky posture, elegant look, well-proportioned model, bright and simple colored together characterize it. Both Indian and Western Lands Buddhist arts greatly influence the sculpture, seat and fineries of it.

Maitreya, the Sanskrit, is freely translated into "Ci Shi", the surname, being born in a Brahmanic family in ancient India and becoming a Buddhist monk latterly. The legend goes that it's an actual person and event. His death was prior to that of Buddha. He lives in Doushuai Palace, expounds to Devas the Buddhist doctrine in character of Bodhisattva and releases all the living from sufferings. He gives priority to the compassion of Buddha's four noble truths of compassion, sadness, happiness and sacrificing oneself. This compassion doctrine comes from the feature of Buddha's speciation doctrine. It can keep the species to raise up seed so that be called " Ci Shi" or" Ci Shi" Bodhisattva. As stated in sculptures that Sakyamuni ever foretold that Maitreya would be born to become Buddha under the Naga-puspa and expound and carry forward Buddhism in place of him while his 4000th birthday coming (i.e. fifty-seven billion and sixty million years in the world), hereby, he is call the complementary Bodhisattva or unborn Buddha, this parlance results in two kinds of sculptures, known as paunchy Maitreya or Cross-legged Maitreya. As recorded in "No.51 section of Unique class of Vol. 49 Agamas Sutra" that Buddha was born and named as Maitreya, Zhizheng, Perfect universal awareness, Sugata, Wiser, Lokavid, Anuttara, Master of devas. He would be Buddha, bless, protect and moralize the world. The elderly thought that it's not the earthling to collect these valuable scriptures in those days, in their eyes that the monk who took the ceremony at that time became the Master nowadays. The emperor donated large quantities of treasures and being accompanied by ministers and other officials to listen to Maitreya and entered into religion because of Maitreya's merits, virtues and wisdom after becoming the Buddha.

Maitreya, in Buddhist sutras, is a historical character; a Buddha come of Bodhisattva; an unborn Buddha to carry forward Buddhism, release all the living from sufferings in place of Sakyamuni and the indication of nice future. Maitreya's doctrine prevails in India, states all over the Western Lands so much as China owing to people's hopes for a nice and bright future.

Bodhisattvas, Cave 419, the Sui Dynasty

Bodhisattvas in Cave 419

Sakyamuni, the host of Cave 419, is accompanied by Kasyapa generally standing at Buddha's nearside and known as the oldest age and be good at his self-torture among Buddha's ten disciples, being awarded "master of discipline"; Anada at Buddha's starboard and being distinguished for his youngest age and cleverness, being awarded "master of hearing and remembering Buddhist doctrine". The murals are foil and supplementary to grottoes. The Bodhisattva's portraits or statues stand by the side of both the Kasyapa and Anada. Bodhisattva can be "self-knowledge" and "for others", but to be not as perfectly good as Buddha's successful end. They would become Buddha after further cultivating themselves according to the religious doctrine.

The sequence of those in niches tells the followings: both kasyapa and Anada's political status and their seating arrangements related to the self-cultivation are below Buddha's but prior to that of Bodhisattva. As the Buddhist "Great Yana" and "Small Yana" says that the capability of the Buddha's ten chief disciples differs with each other. Each of them is master of one power or gift, Sariputras of wisdom; Maudgalyayana of supernatural powers; Mahakasyapa of discipline; Aniruddha of deva vision; Subhuti of explaining the void or immaterial; Purna of preaching the law; Katyayana of its fundermental principlines; Upali of maintaining the rules; Rahula of the esoteric practise and Anada of hearing and remembering. They are able assistants of Sakyamuni, they carry forward the Buddhist doctrine and to be regarded the family dependants. Their status in Buddhism is below Buddha's but above that of Bodhisattva. Kasyapa's whole name is "Maha kasyapa", means " big Kasyapa", standing first among Buddha's ten disciples and being awarded "master of discipline" for his self-torture. The legend goes that Kasyapa is not only the first monk to be handed down the Buddhist scriptures after Buddha's nirvana, but also the convener to collect, compile and record sutras in place of passing on through oral instruction. His face, being experienced and prudent, is bearing with achivement of being the Buddha's favorite disciple. It is an absolute fact that he is not an undernourished disciplinant suffered from self-torture but a robust old monk roamed about though his exposed collarbone and breastbone could be seen clearly. The foreign monk's image of merge face and senility as well as that of Chinese monk's pious and resolute spirit together characterize him. Both Kasyapa and Anada statues in Cave 419 are regarded as the famous painted ones. Anada, being called Anada fully, childish, good looks, elegance in appearance as well as big head, eyes, red nose and being small in stature together characterize him, stands at the south of the western wall in the cave, wears cassock and sackcloth shoes, holds lotus flower in his both hands as gently as a child looking after his treasured toy. The sharp contrast between him and Kasyapa comes forth. The existent Anada's statue in Dunhuang art first appeared in the Northern Zhou regime and ended at the Song Dynasty. Anada's childish image of clever and graceful, big head and round eyes, being small in stature and mouth, gentle, cultivated and piety, listening to the Buddhist doctrines open-mindedly can be found from early statue of those days. The Anada's youthful image of folding hands before his belly, slightly smiling and wiggly waist, comely and rakish, knowing and religious in appearance prevailed since the Tang Dynasty.

Anada, Cave 427, the Sui Dynasty

Merchants Meeting Bandits, Cave 45, the High Tang Dynasty

Merchants Encountering Bandits in Cave 45

Cave 45, one of representative grottoes of the Tang Dynasty, truncated pyramid-shaped top and excavated in the High Tang Dynasty. The statues of Paryankabandha Buddha, Kasyapa, Annada, Kwan-yin, Mahasthama as well as Southern Maharaja and Northern Maharaja are at the niche situated at the western wall of primary hall. Being true to life and high fidelity characterize painted sculptures here and to be regarded as the elaborate works of the High Tang Dynasty. An illustration of Sukhavativyuna-sutra was painted on northern wall and that of Kwan-yin's universals on southern wall respectively and where Kwan-yin's male portrait being centered, he wears gamopetalous crown and is accompanied on both sides by illustrations of his 33 forms and Buddhist stories related to his releasing people out of danger or difficulty. Stories are as follows: merchants encountering bandits, shipwreck, prison, praying for son and finally getting as well as for daughter and finally getting. They reflect the worldly living and customs of the Tang Dynasty, of which, the illustration of merchants encountering bandits catches people's eyes particularly.

Three bandits holding knifes in their hands suddenly jumped out while a group of foreign merchants together with their trade caravan passed by a valley. The merchants wore white fur terais and round collar liveries. They were threatened to surrender treasures and goods. Some of them grimaced in pain or to be in a blue funk, some put on a show of composedness, some closed eyes and put the palms together to pray for Kwan-yin for blessing so much as the donkeys pricked up their ears. The difficulty living and dangerous situation of foreign merchants who came-and-went both Middle and West Asia via the Silk-road is vividly depicted. The illustrative words above the central section of the illustration come out of "Saddharmapundarika-Kwan-yin's universals(a significant Buddhist doctrine) that " merchants would be released from robbery and be safe together with their treasures and goods if they mumble the name and alias of Kwan-yin Bodhisattva while encountering the bandits on the way". This illustration was finished in the period of Kaiyuan and Tianbao of the Emperor Tang Xuanzong's reign, a hoped-for period of joy, serenity, prosperity, and justice. It shows merchants coming and going along the Silk-road would risk encountering the robbers and risk their treasures and goods even if being in millenarianism.

Numerous characters could be found in the illustration of Kwan-yin's universals whose composition being compact; fine and smooth in technique as well as bright-colored and still being kept in actual existence. To believe in Kwan-yin Bodhisattva prevailed in common people in Dunhuang region in the Tang Dynasty owing to thousand-hand and eye Kwan-yin Bodhisattva comes to rescue them as requested while people mumble his name and alias or encountering dangerousness.

Silk-painted Abolokitesvara

Abolokitesvara's portrait, being 80.5cm tall and 53.8cm wide, unearthed at Sutras-Stored Grotto, made of the silk and painted in the High Tang Dynasty, has beige grounding with rosy clouds pattern on its top left corner and pavilions and gallery on clouds which symbolizes Pure Land, on top right corner of it, words "Abolokitesvara" written in Chinese ink can be seen.

Both Abolokitesvara and the soul of a deceased lady were painted. Plump in form, beard and haired, holding a censer in his right hand and lotus stem in his left hand on it the long narrow flag being hung to evoke the dead, standing on lotus and slightly looking back where a well-dressed lady following in the rear, those characterize the Abolokitesvara. The lady to be all-round in form, pretty eyebrows and cerise lips, filigree hair, tamed and obedient and looking as if to be released from the world and on her way to the western Pure Land step by step under Abolokitesvara's guidance.

In Buddhist teaching, the soul of the dead will never die out along with his body. The two destinations await his soul according to his doings above ground as follows: either going to Abaddon to receive sufferings or to the paradise to enjoy life under Abolokitesvara's guidance. As a result of it, the custom of inviting Buddhist monks to do relevant ceremonies for the dead so that he or she could go to paradise prevails, and as time passes, a fixed style " Wang Wen" had come of it, namely making vow before Buddha so that the dead' soul could have a good end-result. As recorded in a "Funeral Oration to Deceased Parent " found in the document of No. S·1441 that "the abyss of misery is impermanent for those lived with six plague spots of eye, ear, nose, tongue, body and mind. The samsara is endless for birth, suffering, death, and rebirth. Life and death go by destiny and happen to all even if ascending ten fairy directions and entering into religion. Those who make vows before Buddha together with other family numbers hope their parent to go to Pure Land and to be far away from six plague spots, having the loud and clear mind for spring and summer, living forever and never grew old just as pine trees in autumn and winter, hoping to be relatives in a future life and praying for Buddha blessing both the alive and the dead. It's a bit too abstraction to express household wish for the dead by aid of words because common people are objects to be moralized on. The illustration of Abolokitesvara guiding soul of a deceased lady to the western Pure Land would influence personnel greatly and they would be gifted with an extraordinarily retentive memory of it owing to their shortage of cultural knowledge in Feudal society.

Many paintings unearthed at Sutras—Stored Grotto can rarely be found in cave murals, for example the illustration of Abolokitesvara. They, being supplements to cave murals, constitute the contents of Buddhist art importantly and show the integrality of Dunhuang Buddhist art together with the cave murals.

Abolokitesvara, a silk painting, the Tang Dynasty

Hong Bian and Noble Woman, Cave 17, the Tang Dynasty

Sutras-Stored Grotto and Hong Bian

The Cave 17 of Mogao grottoes, as it does, is the Sutras-Stored Grotto known to all. WanYuan-lu, come from Hubei and retired from Suzhou Patrol Army in the time of the emperor QingGuang-xu's regime, became a Taoist in Dunhuang owing to the poverty and renamed the lower temple at the Sutras-Stored Grotto's side where he lodged the Shangqing Temple (Taoist temple). Three temples of upper, mid and lower temples were at Mogao Grotto in those days, of which, both upper and middle ones for Lamaist to live and the lower one for WanYuan-lu to cultivate himself and do religious ceremonies. One day, a person with "Yang" to be his surname and hired himself to WanYuan-lu to copy Taoist scriptures, "Yang" inserted a splendid achnatherum being used to light a fire while smoking into a wall slit omnivorously, to his astonishment that he could not insert it into the end of the slit, he knocked at the wall and perceived that it's hollow just beyond the wall. "Yang" told WanYuan-lu what he found. They broke the wall that night and entered into the grotto where filled with large quantities of calico bundles arranged orderly. Tens of sutras in different number and category were found in every bundle. Spread Buddhist flags, embroidered portraits and silk paintings could be found in those bundles together with 40,000 volumes of ancient hand-copied books, block-printed editions, paper paintings, silk paintings as well as musical instruments used in a Buddhist mass and offerings, etc. of the dynasties from the Wei, Jin to the Early Song Dynasties. They were amazed and excited to find those treasures. With regard to the discovery of Scripture-Stored Grotto, the "Record related to rebuilding Tri-storied Building of the Thousand Buddha Grotto inscribed on the merit tablet" being put up in 1906 and inlaid the southern wall of the paved path leading to No.16 grotto says that "in the first month of the summer of 1900, another grotto filled with numerous Buddhist sutras and copper statues of Buddha in company with a tablet being engraved the inscription of "being put up by HongBian, a Buddhist monk, in the 5th year of Dazhong in the Tang Dynasty(i.e.851)" was found beyond the grotto wall to the north. As WanYuan-lu recorded that " in the morning of May 26 in the 6th year of the emperor QingGuang-xu's regime, a grotto's wall split suddenly along with the thunderclap and then the Scripture-Stored Grotto was found". The discovery of Sutras-Stored Grotto, unrivalled ancient precious deposits, is regarded as one of the greatest discoveries in the 20th century. It's great luck for both Chinese and international academias. Unfortunate to them, some other countries plundered them as soon as showing their faces owing to weak Chinese fate and big powers rule the region in those days.

Cave16, tri-storied, is the merit grotto of HongBian who had ever been the vice instructor, the head of instructors when the ancient Tibetan dominating Dunhuang region as well as the head of monk officials in charge of Buddhist matters concerned in Hexi region after ZhangYi-chao had recaptured it in the 5th year of Dazhong in the Tang Dynasty (i.e.851). HongBian, being benevolent, versed in Buddhism and developing Buddhist monks and nuns, was an unwonted master in the Dunhuang's Buddhist history. He contributed all his life to carrying forward Buddhism in Dunhuang region and excavated grottoes in large numbers there within tens of years in succession. The existent Scripture—Stored Grotto, the HongBian's Zendo before his death where he sat in meditation and self-cultivated, becomes a hall where HongBian's statue being situated in memory of his merits. In Cave17, double trees were painted at the northern wall together with a female attendant standing under the leftward tree, holding walking stick and hand towel in her hands and a bag hung on the tree and as well as with a nun standing under the rightward tree, holding a fan in here hands and a water jug hung on the tree. The kindly and tranquil statue of his sitting in meditation was centered and accompanied by the painting of double deer holding flower in the mouths and lion at the south of bed as well as the painting of a pair of shoes at the north. He seemed to be encircled by sutras and enter into Pure Land. HongBian's merit tablet in Cave 17 was engraved and then inlaid the grotto wall in the 5th year of Dazhong in the Tang Dynasty (i.e.851) after HongBian being entitled "the head of monk officials of Hexi region". The trace of tablet-inlaid still can be seen clearly. HongBian, the saintly master, his meditation statue in memory of him was molded and seated by his disciples and believers. It took place not long after the 3rd year of Weitong of the Tang Dynasty(i.e.862).

Playing Zither and Illustration of Requiting Kindness Sutra

Illustration of Requiting kindness's sutra, painted in 28 grottoes in Mogao Grotto, first appeared in Cave 148 in the High Tang Dynasty, gradually increased in number and continued to the Song Dynasty latterly. It's drawn basing upon "Mahopaya Buddha's Requiting Kindness" which employs 9 classes of 7 volumes as follows: No.1: Introducting chaptter; No.2:XiaoYang; No.3: DuiZhi; No.4: Vowing to devote the mind to bodi; No.5:LunYi; No.6: A friend in bad life; No.7:CiPin; No.8: Rahula; No.9: QinJin. The rest parts with exception of YouPoli which narrating mitzvahs relate to following themes: giving the filial piety to parent and loyalty to master as well as returning good for evil and being concious of a kindness and acknowledging a duty to repay it, as to this content, the parts such as No.1, No.2, No.5, No.6 and No. 7 are involved; another theme relates to persuading people to believe in Buddhism and reach an immortal state, such as stated in No.3, No.4, No.7 and No.9 items. 100-odd illustration's contents found in Mogao Grotto deal with those 9 parts. The "illustration of requiting kindness's sutra", in fact, advocates to repaying the Buddha's kindness firstly, the sovereign and parent's kindness secondly and then the kindness of the common people, of which, it gives priority to the second one. The Hans's sovereigns, since the Han Dynasty, respected Confucianism the lineal doctrine, emphasized to give filial piety to parent firstly, loyalty to sovereign secondly and establish oneself finally. The sovereigns of past Dynasties took "filial piety" as the grounded theory to educate common people and rule over the country, in the meanwhile, fully ensured and supported it in politics, legislation and education, etc. The peculiar ethics, political and legal concept as well as Buddhist doctrine jointly constituted the ancient Chinese thought owing to the ancient sovereigns advocating and combining Confucian doctrine of filial piety with Buddhism personally. In Mogao Grotto's murals, the scenes of playing the musical instruments, the sacred work for female musicians, to improve happy atmosphere in Pure Land greatly can be seen everywhere. It's a common female musician in Tang's clothes and played the zither in "illustration of requiting kindness's sutra" in Cave 85 being excavated in the Late Tang Dynasty. Her carefree and content looks actually reflects the situation, being corresponded with the life in the western Pure Land exactly, of developed economy, being on easy street as well as people living and working in peace and contentment in the Late Tang Dynasty. The spectacle of Pure Land came from people's image owing to conscience of a kindness and acknowledging a duty to repay it. The true-life spectacle people created can be more happy and prosperous that that in Pure Land. The picture of zither somewhat similar to a twenty-five-stringed plucked instrument can be seen in Cave 297 being excavated in the Northern Zhou, it's named zither basing upon relevant records in "Sui Shu(History of the Sui Dynasty)" and other documents because Chinese ancient "se(twenty-five-stringed plucked instrument)" had died out actually as from the dynasties of the Jin, Southern and Northern, Sui and Tang. The musical instruments played by female musicians in " the Western Liang", "Qiuci", etc. were not called "se", in addition, as recorded in "YiWenLeiJu· No.41 section ·Musical Instruments" that the zithers used in both Bing and Liang prefectures were somewhat similar to "se" and nobody knew the producer of them. Both zither and "se" are stringed and plucked musical instruments, no other substantial difference exists between them except for the zither's string number being less than that of "se". YanShugu's "Comments" of "JiJiuPian" as well as "Jiu Tang Shu (Old History of the Tang Dynasty)· Musical Record" said that the zither, being the orchestral music with rapid and rich rhythm, employing 12 strings originally, but 13ones nowadays, belonged in the field of "se".

Playing the zither under a tree, the southern wall, Cave 85, the Late Tang Dynasty

The zithers found in both Bing and Liang prefectures only held the original shape and structure of "se" and were not reformed intentionally. The music, being thought of the non-objectivism and the art of sense of hearing, can heart-quake and excite listener's soul and relieve them from their fatigues and over-anxiety. The purpose of practicing the Buddhism teachings aims at enjoying oneself and overcome one's desires as well as being pure-hearted and molding temperament. The spectacle of playing zither under a tree not only reflects the rich material and spiritual life in those days but also to be thought of the better way to cultivate oneself.

Bodhisattva, Cave 57, the Early Tang Dynasty

Bodhisattva in Cave 57

Bodhisattva mural in Cave 57 is the magnum opus of Tang's murals. The center of the grotto's magnificent caisson ceiling is painted double dragons accompanied by lotus flower, curtains spreading around and Flying Devi flying about. The statues of a Paryankabandha Buddha (i.e.to sit cross-legged), his two principle disciples and four Bodhisattvas are situated at the both outer and inner arched niches on the western wall. The wall of inner niche employs flamy lotus halo surrounding the head and back of a Buddha together with a Buddha's disciple and a Flying Devi at its both sides as well as flamy lotus lintel at the ceiling of outer niche and Flying Devi at its both sides. On both sides of the western wall are painted niche columns and two Meditating Bodhisattvas. On both southern and northern walls are painted Bodhisattva respectively. Six Flying Devi figures, flying towards the offering below the niche in opposite directions, are painted in the niche. The three Offering Bodhisattvas are painted at both sides of the offering respectively. The story related to Sakyamuni over-flying the town wall at night to study the doctrine is painted at the upside of the south out of the niche in company with two Bodhisattvas in the middle part and two attendant Bodhisattvas at the under part. The story about Sakyamuni riding an elephant to enter into his mother's belly is painted at the upside of the north out of the niche in company with two Bodhisattvas in the middle part and two attendant Bodhisattvas at the under part. Both southern and northern walls are painted thousand Buddha together with the chart of expounding Buddhist doctrine centered on it and donors stood in row at the under part; the donors of the later pertained to time of the Late Tang Dynasty. The eastern wall's door, with charts of thousand Buddha and expounding Buddhist doctrine at its upside and under part respectively, is painted thousand Buddha at the upside and the seven Buddha of the Early Tang Dynasty at the under part(being destroyed at the time of the Late Tang Dynasty while building the paved path leading to a main hall).

Cave 57, known as one of representative grottoes of the earlier stage of the Early Tang Dynasty, alias "grotto of a queen of hearts" for 20-odd graceful Bodhisattva figures there. The most graceful figure is situated at the east side of "Amitabha expounding Buddhist doctrine"being centered on the southern wall. Kwan-yin Bodhisattva, egg-shaped face, fine eyebrows and eyes, upright nose and small lips exposed neck, wearing gamopetalous crown, waist made of beautiful brocade, magnificent skirt, necklace, jade-like stones, armlet, bracelets and jade pendant (worn on a girdle). She looks richly bejeweled with luxuriant costumes. Kwan-yin Bodhisattva slightly raises her one hand near the chain and another drooping behind the body together with her bare-feet on big lotus flowers, her waist slightly presents S-shape, slightly tilted head and looks musingly. The graceful statures and lifelike expression together with the above mentioned characterize it, one of the most graceful Kwan-yin Bodhisattva portraits in the Tang Dynasty.

Kwan-yin Bodhisattva in her portrait has slender stature, slightly tilted body, to be true to life. Slightly protuberant belly has sense of reality and springiness. Looking down slightly, quiet and gentle expression, implicative but missish beauty together constitute here features. The Tang's Bodhisattva portraits, laying stress on portraying the character of personality and tracing out the Bodhisattva's motion by aid of natural and facile lines, differ with that of the Sui Dynasty which emphasizing Bodhisattva's character by the help of coarse lines, exaggerated and transmutative technique. The motional depiction richly displays the Bodhisattva's psychosis and merciful or compassionate nature. The seeking for gaudiness breaks through the restriction of the religion, the art image, hereon, moves up to the freedom bourn.

Buddha's Nirvana, Cave 158, the Mid-Tang Dynasty

The recumbent Buddha's statue in Cave158, 16m in stature, being sculptured in the Tang Dynasty according to the story of Sakyamuni lying between two Saltrees nearby the Bati river in Jushina city to enter into nirvana, lies on the Buddhist altar on the western wall in the main hall and seems to be fell asleep with the characteristic of wavy hair worn in a big bun, neither close nor open eyes as well as the serene and gratified smile because of two sides of his nose and deep-set corners of the mouth being sculptured in intaglio. The neck's tri-level wrinkles make his plump skin stand out. The cassock worn covers his whole body closely and changes along with stature naturally, the Tang's appreciation of the rich and gaudy as well as plump beauty thus can be seen. The strong expression in the murals related to 72 disciples going into mourning brightly stands in vivid contrast against Sakyamuni's serene and graceful look. Sakyamuni's nirvana statue is one of outstanding works kept in actual existence in Mogao Grotto.

Three statues of "Past Buddha" standing on the southern wall, "Current Buddha" on the western wall as well as "Future Buddha" on the northern wall are generally called "Three-periods Buddha". As stated in sutrs that "lifetime being torment and nirvana the pleasure", the great pleasure will come after one's death and the soul of the dead will enter into Pure Land only after one's body dieing out. As to the Bodhisattvas, Arhat, Deva, Naga and those eight classes of supernatural beings in the lotus sutra who protecting Buddhist doctrine, they went into mourning over Sakyamuni. Arhat has just attained enlightenment and in Buddhist world is not as highly noble-minded as Bodhisattva who to be leniency and rescues the common people from the torment and tribulation; as a result of it, as to the nirvana of Buddha, Bodhisattva's impervious expression shows he is in a higher moral stature, by contraries, Arhat's crying his heart out shows that he does not understand Buddha's nirvana really. The princes from different countries went into mourning for Buddha's nirvana, some of them committed to cut their ears and noses, some cried their eyes out, some so much as committed suicide owing to deep sorrow, these scenes vividly reflect the devotional religious sentiment of the Buddhists in the Western Lands. They are important for researching and understanding their habits and customs as well as trappings.

Recumbent Buddha Statue in Cave 158

As stated in Buddhist doctrine that life is agonizing and nirvana is happy. The nirvana denotes to practice Buddhism and grasp the truth, reach samadhi, disengage oneself from the torment of birth, old age, illness and death as well as transmigration and enter into Pure Land where no birth and death except for the boundless joyousness. This Buddhist teaching resulted in the establishment of Sakyamuni's nirvana statue there.

The illustration of Sakyamuni's nirvana sutra in Cave 158 shows the magnificent scene of attending the Sakyamuni's funeral as follows: 12 Buddhist monks carrying luxuriant inner and outer coffins, holding pennants, streamers as well as censers and flowers to go to Jhpeti (i.e. crematorium) accompanied by all disciples in heavenly-minded atmosphere. The Eight Kings (Youtian, Murdhaja-raja, Ersheng, Ajiatasatru, Zuihao, Rongyi, Zhishen and Jingang) crossed the Ganges River and came to scrabble for Buddha's relic in Kusinagara city one after another while hearing of it. They, wearing various fur caps or terais as well as campaign gowns, holding pikes and shields, riding war horses, fought closely. A king dropped dead because of being badly wounded. The chain of mountains in the distance together with the torrential Ganges River made the blood-and-thunder atmosphere between funeral ceremony and wars stand out. Sakyamuni, to be dead before long, was being lying there serenely, perceiving his disciple's grieved howls by his deva ears and looking at this combative battlefield containedly by his deva eyes. He had disengaged himself from various torments and fatigues and entered into Pure Land.

Group of Painted Clay Figures, Cave 45, the High Tang Dynasty

Group of Painted Clay Figures in Cave45

Cave 45, excavated in the High Tang Dynasty, truncated pyramid-shaped top with a niche situated on the western wall. The Five Dynasties' mural of Thousand Hand and Eye's Kwan-yin centers on the top of front hall together with a Five-Dynasties' mural of Kwan-yin on the south side and a Five-Dynasties' mural of Talismanic wheel Kwan-yin on the north side of it. The western wall's door employs a Five-Dynasties' mural related to Pishamen's Maharaja attending Nata Buddhist meeting together with Five-Dynasties' illustration of sutra remained at the south and north of the door respectively. Only one corner of Five-Dynasties' illustration of sutra remains on the southern wall as well as that of Hua-yen sutra remains on the northern wall. The murals of Buddhist historical sites together with Five-Dynasties' images of Buddha can be seen respectively at the wooden box-shaped top center as well as the north and south of the corridor. At the primary hall's magnificent caisson ceiling, lotus flowers are painted together with curtains spreading around on which thousand Buddha being painted. Seven statues of Paryankabandha Buddha, Kasyapa, Annada, Kwan-yin, Mahasthama as well as Southern Maharaja and Northern Maharaja are at the flat-topping and unstricted niche being situated on the western wall in the primary hall. At the top and bottom of the niche are painted stupa and Bodhi canopy respectively in company with two High Tang's Bodhisattva images being painted at both sides of Buddha's true light shined upon the niche wall, images of Ti-tsang and that of Kwan-yin are painted at the north and south sides out of the niche respectively. The High Tang's illustrations of Kwan-yin sutra and Kwan-yin's Sukhativyuha-sutra are painted on the southern and northern walls respectively. No mural at eastern wall's door except for a Mid-Tang's image of Ti-tsang and that of Kwan-yin are painted at the north and a High Tang's image of Kwan-yin Bodhisattva at the south of it.

The front and primary halls constitute this grotto. Cassocked Kasyapa, The features of cassocked, wide forehead, knitted bushy eyebrows and closed lips make Kasyapa's great learning and great ability stand out. Annada, slightly bends stature with obedient looks, listens to the Buddhist doctrine open-mindedly and stands just as Buddha's boy. 1.85m tall in stature, hair worn in a big bun, round face, wearing jade-like stones, armlet and bracelets as well as looking down and lovely expression and S-shaped stature characterize the statue of Bodhisattva who is listening to the Buddha edification respectfully. The Cave45's painted clay figures are the magnum opus of statuaries of the High Tang Dynasty.

Painted Clay Sculpture, Bodhisttva, Cave 45, the Tang Dynasty

Bodhisattva Kasyapa and Lokaoala, Cave 45, the High Tang Dynasty

Musicians and Dancers in the Palace of Devas, Cave 249, the Western Wei Dynasty

Flying Devi Figures

Flying Devi, legendary those protect Buddhist doctrine in the Hinduism, and to be the combination of Gandharvas and Kinnara. As stated in Article 11 of "Dinctionary of sounds and meanings of Buddhist wors and phrases" that Kinnara is the performer in heavenly palace, being capable of singing and dancing, being horse-headed and man-bodied for male performers as well as pretty human body for female performers, the most of them became the wife of Gandharvas. The Vol.10 of "Sastra on the Prajiana-paramita sutra" says that Gandharvas had ever been the performer of Devas. Among Deva, Naga and other eight classes of supernatural beings in the lotus sutra, He presided at presenting fresh flowers to Buddha, emitted aroma, provided offerings, read sutras and did divine services. He could stay in flowers and fly in heaven palace. Kinnara, living in the heaven palace but being unable to fly in sky, answered for playing music, doing performance for Buddha, Bodhisattvas as well as all Devas in Pure Land. Their duties lately became in one and they turned into the flying Devi.

The number of Flying Devi in Mogao Grotto is acclaimed a marvel. According to statistics that 4500-odd images of Flying Devi are found in over 270 ones of the total 492 Magao Grottoes except for those being found in Yulin, Eastern and Western Thousand Buddha Grottoes. Adding these figures together, total over 6000 in number can be seen everywhere. The biggest Flying Devi image found in main Buddhist hall of Cave130 is over 2m long, by contraries, the smallest one ranges between 5 to 6cm. Total 156 Flying Devi images, the greatest quantity for a single grotto, are found in Cave 209. Mural, clay sculpture, brick carving and stone inscription constitute the Flying Devi artistic form owing to specific geographical conditions. Of which, the forenamed mural, clay sculpture, brick carving can often be seen in Hexi region, and the stone inscription happens commonly to Yungang Cave, Longmeng and Dazu Grottoes. The Flying Devi artistic image appeared in murals along with the beginning excavation of Mogao Grotto, and continued for 1000-odd years running from the year of 366 to 1368. Cave 329 with its caisson ceiling on a sky-blue background which symbolizing the sky was excavated in the Early Tang Dynasty. The luxuriantly bloomed lotus accompanied by four Flying Devi images centers on the caisson ceiling. They, in various postures, flutter among the flowers with their long silk streamers flying over with the breeze. 12 female performers fly and play various musical instruments around the outside ring of the caisson ceiling. Flying Devi, alias "gods of fragrance and music", they fly in the sky and give out fresh flowers while Buddha expounding Buddhist doctrine. The sky is permeated with a dedicate fragrance while they are away. The four images on the upside of the Pure Land's illustration, the most beautiful Flying Devi images in Mogao Grotto, are magnum opus of them. They symmetrically fly in two equal groups and change postures occasionally. As for the right group, a Flying Devi flys ahead in a posture of spreading hands relaxedly, turns her head back to give out flower petals larkishly, the open-armed latter one gathers herself together to fly and tries to catch up with the former in a posture of stretching out her right legs at full tilt. Dunhuang's Flying Devi who flying airily and imaginably by the aid of long silk streamers differs from the Angel who flying freely with the aid of her wings in the West oil painting. Dunhuang's Flying Devi excites common people greatly.

The Flying Devi in murals appeared as early as the excavation of Mogao Grotto, continued for over 1000 years of ten-odd Dynasties from the 16-States to the Yuan Dynasty and died out along with the stop excavation of Mogao Grottoes as late as the last years of the Yuan Dynasty. Their image, posture as well as artistic conception, spice of art and style occasionally changed along with the regime's supersession, economical development, frequent cultural interflow between ancient China and the west. The unique development history of Dunhuang's Flying Devi image formed during over 1000years is consistent with Dunhuang's artistic development history in the rough. Their four ages are as follows: Arisen Age: about 170 years in number starting from the Northern Liang to Northern Wei of 16-States(i.e. the year of 336 to535), the period during which the Flying Devi image took Western Lands style or pattern owing to being greatly influenced by both Indian and the Western Lands's Flying Devi. Innovative Age: about 80 years in number starting from the Western Wei to Sui Dynasty(i.e. the year of 535 to 618), the period during which the Flying Devi image employed the combination of Chinese and Western relevant style or pattern owing to the close interflow between Buddhist Flying Devi and Taoist winged Deva as well as Western Lands's Flying Devi and central plains' fairy. Silver

Flying devi, Cave 285, the Western Wei Dynasty

Age: about300 years in number starting from the Early Tang to Late Tang Dynasty (i.e. the year of 618 to970), the period during which the highest point of the Flying Devi image art is attained with the little Indian pattern could be seen except for the simplex Chinese style. Winter Age: about 460 years in number starting from the Five Dynasties to Yuan Dynasty (i.e. the year of 970 to 1368), the period during which Flying Devi image art only succeeded to Tang's aftertaste, innovate nothing in its formation except for formulization, both Sui's innovation and Tang's style of pressing forward could never be seen unfortunately. Flying Devi image art became declining and lost their artistic livingness length by length though their artistic level and style ever differing.

As for the artistic image of Flying Devi grown up and developed under the carefully and jointly fostering of Indian, Silk-road as well as the Western Lands and central plains' culture though being derived from India, both the onefold art image and the combination of multi-culture characterize it. It can say that Dunhuang's Flying Devi images are most outstanding genius of ancient Chinese artists. Their elegant movements and postures stand in vivid contrast against quiet Buddha images, add great vital force to the grottoes, solemnify the scene of Buddha's expounding Buddhist doctrine as well as enlarge the member of those who listens to and protect Buddhist doctrine and humanize the whole Buddhist rites. It's a miracle happened to the Buddhist history.

One flying devi on the southern wall, Cave 285, the Western Wei Dynasty

Flying devi on the western wall, Cave 158, the Mid-Tang Dynasty

Flying devi on the top of the niche, Cave 419, the Sui Dynasty

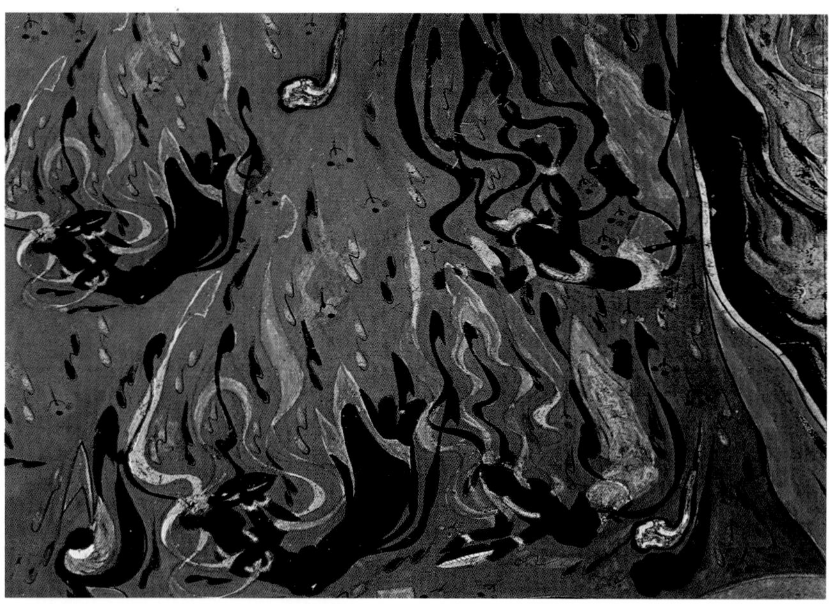

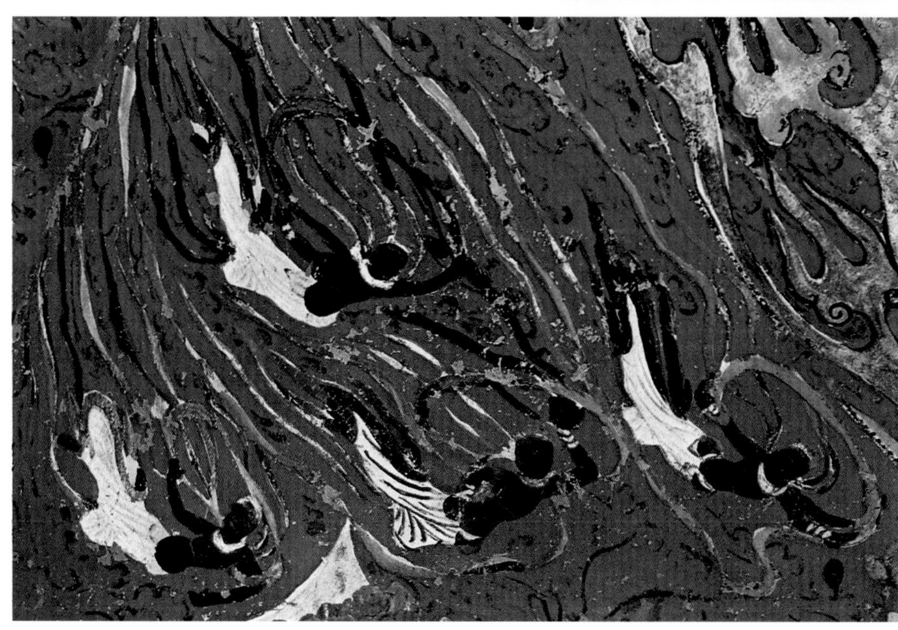

Flying devi, Cave 206, the Sui Dynasty

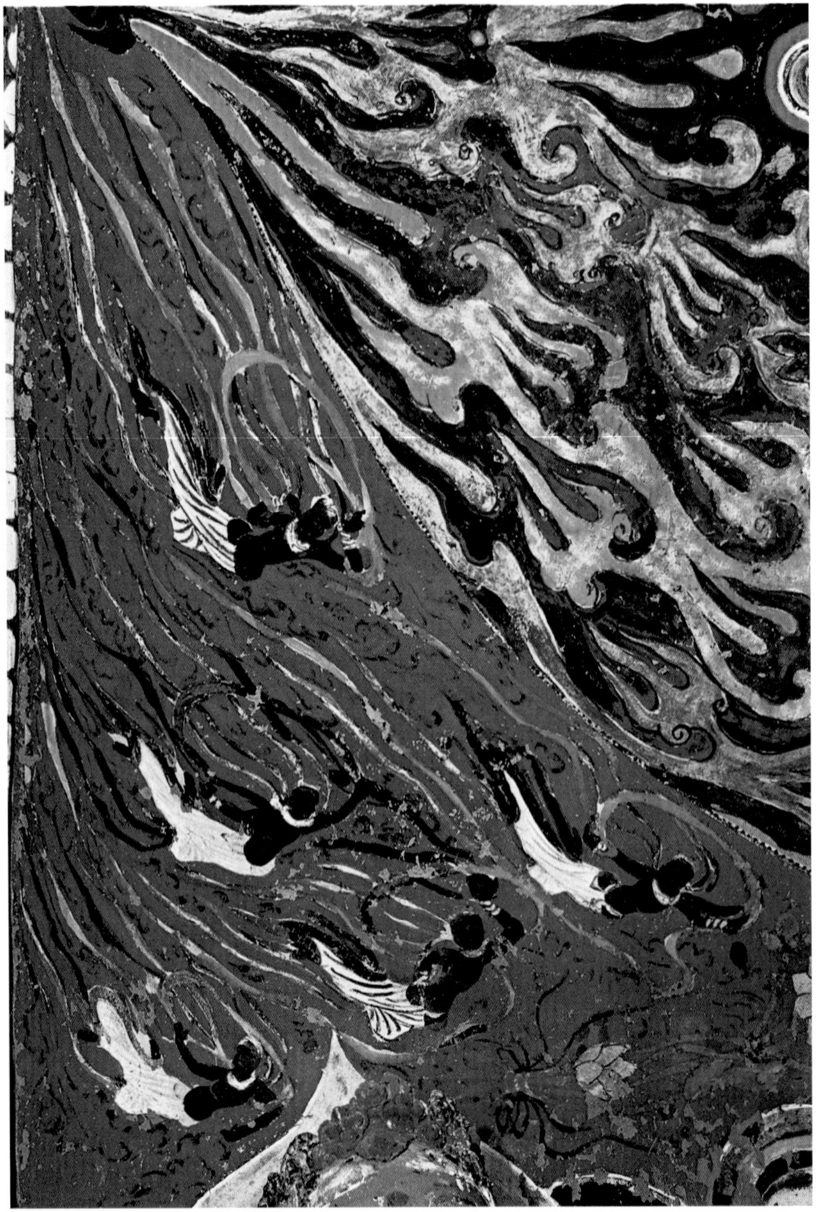

Flying Devi, Cave 206, the Sui Dynasty

Flying Devi on the Top of the Niche, Cave 419, the Sui Dynasty

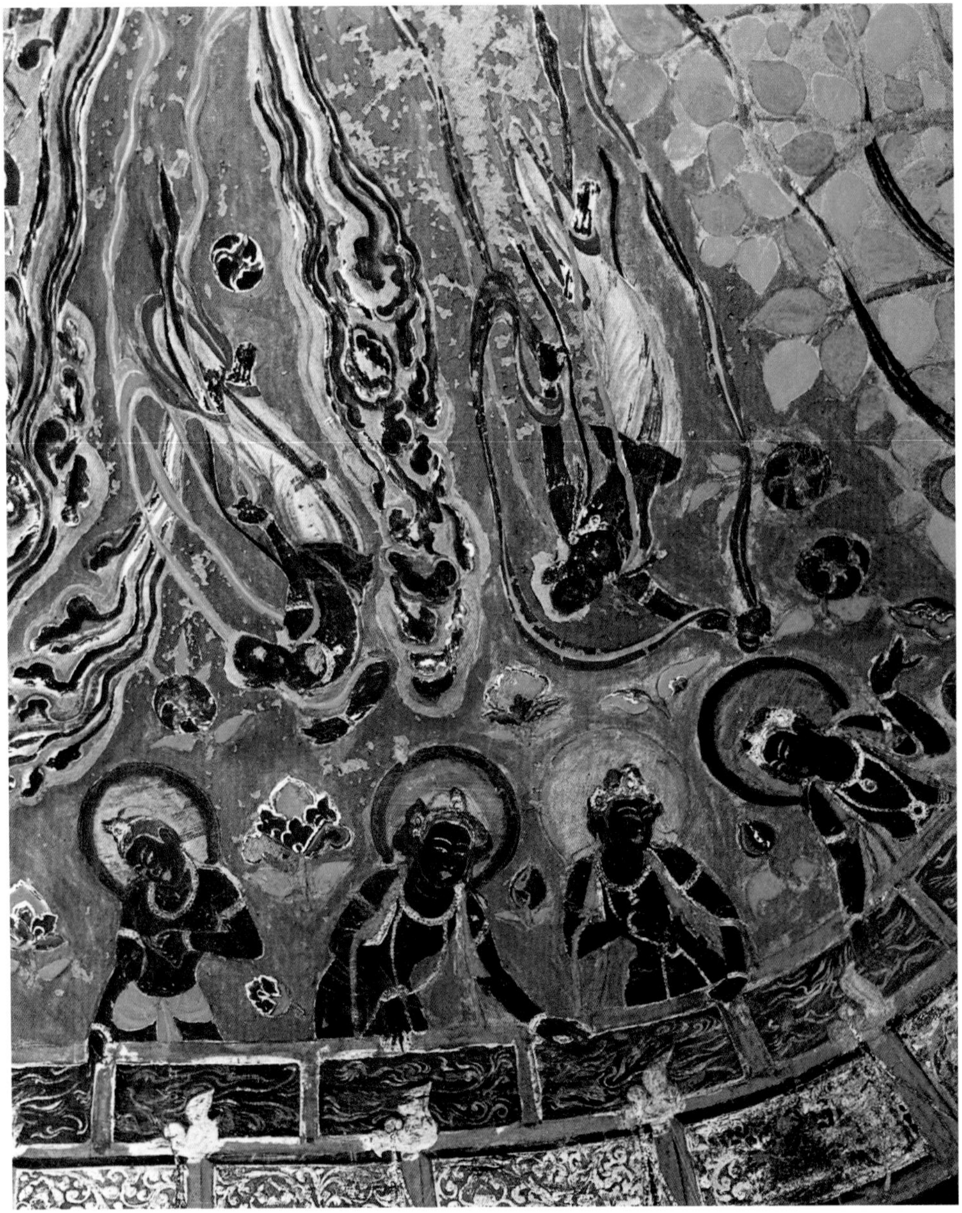

Heavenly Musician and Flying Devi on the Top of the Niche, Cave 321, the Early Tang Dynasty

Double Flying Apsaras, Cave 321, the Early Tang Dynasty

Double Flying Devi, Cave 320, the High Tang Dynasty

Musicians and dancers in the Palace of Devas, Cave 249, the Western Wei Dynasty

Cave 465

Cave 465, alias "Huang" Grotto, one of important grottoes in Mogao Grotto, being distinguished for many double-body images labeled the style of Tibet Buddhism within it and excavated as late as the last years of the Yuan Dynasty, as to its artistic level, is the outstanding one and rare in its artistic value during which period.

Truncated pyramid-shaped front hall, destroyed eastern wall, a stupa being painted on the southern and northern walls as well as the south and north sides of the western wall's door respectively. On the top of it is painted an image of Bodhisattva together with lines of cloudy obscured haze on the corridor top where the painted peony flowers situated at the south and north of it. The truncated pyramid-shaped primary hall has a multistoried and round Buddhist altar centered on it where the original Tibet Buddhist Mandala has disappeared nowadays. The legend goes that the clay sculpture situated at the altar was also a double-body statue and being sent out respectively because of being unfit to be seen. What the murals in Cave 465 reflected relates to the Tibetan Buddhism, of which, the murals painted on top's caisson ceiling and all around show images of "Five wisdoms and Universally penetrating" as follows: Vairocana, Aksobhya, Ratnasambhave, Amitabha and Amoghasiddhi. Mandala's three images, on the western wall, are painted in the following order from the south to north: single-bodied image of Buddha's warrior attendant holding a pestle in hands; double-bodied image of Buddha's warrior attendant holding pestle and bell in hands respectively; single-bodied image of Buddha's warrior attendant holding a knife and a bowl in hands respectively. They had been painted true to life and ever been stolen off in 1989 owing to their fine quality and rare value, they were resumed their seats after the case being solved. Mandala's three images, on the southern wall, are painted in the following order from the east to west: single-bodied image holding a bow and arrow in hands; ox-seated double-bodied image; double-bodied image being wrapped human being's husk around. Twenty or twenty-one round-shaped images are painted around above-mentioned Mandala's images. Mandala's three images, on the northern wall, are painted in the following order from the east to west: seventeen-headed and fourteen armed single-bodied image; the second image being destroyed already; thirty-six armed and mendicant double-bodied image. Twenty small round-shaped images, around each of the above-mentioned, are painted respectively. The image of five Buddha's warrior attendants headed by Mahatejas is painted on the eastern wall's door together with two images of offering monk painted at both sides of it. At the south of the door, a Mandala's image, three groups of Mule Maharaja images as well as four images of Fire Boy are painted, in the meanwhile, such twenty-four images as one Mandala's and Pinayejia, etc. are painted at the north of the door. The original horizontal boards inscribed in both Chinese and Tibetan characters appended to each painting are out of existence nowadays. The working scene of pounding grains, picking tea-leaves and weaving as well as living scene of playing fine musical instruments are important materials for researching the social situation of the Yuan Dynasty.

Vairavesa , Cave 465, the Yuan Dynasty

The attendant Bodhisattva's image, labeled the rich Tibetan Buddhist style and skyscraping art value, in Cave 465 is one of the magnum opuses of the Mogao Grotto's Buddhist arts in the Yuan Dynasty. Wearing pagoda-shaped tri-pearl crown and short skirt; uncovered upper part of the body, both red-dyed palms and soles, wide and protrudent forehead, deep eyeholes, high eyebrows Roma nose, protrudent chin, viewing and admiring the lotus held in hands, the dye happened to the character infrequently, the halo srounding the head and back of Buddha image as well as gilded waistband, elegance and civility together characterize it.

Raudrakasa's Battle with Buddha's Disciple Sariputra

XuDa, a faithful minister of king Posini in ancient India, was a man of wealth and earned a reputation of "Geigudu" owing to his loving to do philanthropic work and at other's service. The six of his seven sons had been married except for the little one. He asked for Brahman, a local of high standing, to introduce a well-content girl to his unmarried son. One day, Brahman reached Wangshe town and was told that HuMi, a minister being access of money to power and beneficent, has a beautiful maid. He visited HuMi and prayed for him to marry his daughter to XuDa's, HuMi promised him owing to XuDa's great reputation and he thought it's matched for the marriage. XuDa was warmly feasted while he took numerous money and valuables to make engagement with HuMi. XuDa, looked at the feast and said to HuMi " it's my luck to enjoy these delicious foods you prepared for your daughter", "No.", HuMi said without more ado, "they are prepared just for greeting Sakyamuni, a sage".

Sakyamuni, being widely eulogized for his sermon and expounding Buddhist doctrine in every state all over the ancient India, expounded Buddhist doctrine to XuDa as soon as he came to HuMi's room when the sun was setting in mountains. XuDa listened to Sakyamuni eagerly and suddenly saw the light. He invited Sakyamuni to expound Buddhist doctrine in Shewei town and even promised to build a luxury teaching room for him. Sakyamuni failed in refusing this great kindness and finally promised his request. XuDa suspended the engagement momentarily and returned Shewei town in company with Sariputra, a disciple of Sakyamuni, to look a right place to build the teaching room, but to their disappointment that no appropriate places can be found except for prince's garden situated in downtown. XuDa's artful words moved the prince to trade it for gold only on condition that the number of the gold should be enough to overspread the whole garden. Sariputra's infinitely resourceful and magic arts satisfied the prince and XuDa got the garden. Unfortunately, an accident happened, Brahman's Raudraksa, a Brahmanist, heard that Sariputra had deceived the prince by the aid of magic arts and threatened to match magical powers with him to look for the winner. One day, the contest happened between them, Raudraksa entered high and mighty, then sat down and held high his head, but Sariputra entered unhurriedly and sat down Raudraksa's nearside, closed his eyes with repose of mind. This battle caught all people's eyes and the king so much as came in person.

The battle began formally, Raudraksa set up for his magic arts being more powerful than that of Sariputra and was sure of success. He suddenly produced a high and steep fairy mountain where to be gloriously radiant, trees are flourishing, all immortals riding cranes, dragons and singing the song to wander about, they wore the audience's unanimous applause. Sariputra sat quietly and neglected audience's eyes, XuDa worried about Sariputra very much. Sariputra produced a warrior to smash the mountain with a pestle held in both hands. Then astonished Raudraksa produced a buffalo, its blare trembled earth and swayed mountains, a lion suddenly jumped from Sariputra and killed the

Raudraksa's battle with Buddha's disciple Sariputra, Cave 196, the Late Tang Dynasty

buffalo; in succession, Sariputra's elephant blotted up the deep water in pond produced by Raudraksa and a beautiful bird with golden wings killed Raudraksa's great viper as well as Pisha Tianmen Wang faced down Raudraksa's two malicious ghosts; finally, Raudraksa, in a blue funk, produced a huge tree, but Sariputra's violent wind plucked it out of root together with Raudraksa's bed-curtain, Raudraksa lost the bell and, candidly admitted the defeat and converted to power of Buddha.

Before long, the teaching room was accomplished and became the Buddhist Holy place after Sakyamuni's expounding Buddhist doctrine there. XuDa, heretofore, remembered his son's marriage, and made haste to send a party to escort that beautiful bride to his son's house.

Siddhartha Getting Over Town wall at Night

Pure rice King (i.e.Suddhodana), Sakyamuni's father, was greatly relieved at the birth of Siddhartha prince when he was old and minded his son carefully in necessities of life. He set his heart on educating Siddhartha prince to be the qualified successor, a man of both civil and military ability as well as possessing both ability and political integrity, to the throne so that he could administer the country and stabilize people's livelihood.

Siddhartha prince, in a flash, was about 20 years old and married. To his father's disappointment, he did not interest in administering national affairs, ran short of joy of living and even being tired of his life. His father was in dread of him and sent him many belles and treasures for the sake of awakening and calling his attention to the future and happy life. His father was not successful because Siddhartha prince concerned and worried about nothing except for the birth, old age, illness and death of the life although his father latterly arranged many cleaver, decorous in appearance, polite and blue-blooded young men to accompany him to help him become aware of the authority as a crown prince. Siddhartha prince thought little of this artificial honor and wealth. He liked to sit under a Yanfu tree alone to meditate on the truth of birth and death, rise and fall as well as uncertainly changeable life and did not like to be disturbed while going out for a tour with others. To overcome illusive youth and haleness, terrible old age, illness and death as well as rescuing the earthling out of the abyss of misery became his only spirit support. He continued his meditation while a monk coming to him. He stood up to greet the monk and asked deferentially: " who are you? why do you dress this strange clothes? "The monk answered: "I' m a monk freed off the tie of my family, I' m tired of the trouble of old age, illness and death of the life, I looked for the way to shake off them and finally found that nobody could escape from that, so I enter into religion where I' m not bothered and I can overcome desires, and to attain enlightenment becomes my only desire." Siddhartha prince was pleased by monk's words, he said to him: " I have the idea same as yours, I'm looking for the way to shake off it, I' m lucky to encounter you here, you show me the way forward and light my dark world." Siddhartha prince found that monk out of his eyes while he finished his words.

Siddhartha prince determined to enter into religion because he thought this adventure as the Past Buddha's transforming him. He returned home and gave goodwill to his father and then he expounded the terrible life and death to his father. He solicited for his father's consent. What Pure rice King worried about had taken place, he wept out: " Please stop your absurd idea, your are prince and successor to the throne, both our country and family need you, my son." Siddhartha prince said to his father very politely that: "Dear father, I will not do that if you can meet my following wishes: No trace of becoming old; No misery of sickness; No trepidation of the death and No damages and disappearance happened to everything on earth." Pure rice King shook his head again and again and said: " My dear son, are you mad£¿How do you say that£¡Nobody can escape from them. You can ascend the throne at once if you stop entering into religion." Siddhartha prince seemed to hear nothing. Pure rice King understood that his son had his decision made, he finally ordered guard soldiers to watch and ward the town against Siddhartha prince's forsaking the world. One night, Siddhartha prince, seizing the chance that maid-in-waiting being weary owing to the long time musical performance, asked his attendant to lead his white horse, he would cultivated himself according to a religious doctrine in mountains. Unfortunately, the closed town gate blocked his way at night and troubled him. A light suddenly appeared in the sky while he felt puzzled, four Devas came down the light and lifted white horse's hooves and overflew the town wall. Siddhartha prince, herefrom, was on the way to shake off the abyss of misery.

Siddhartha getting over the wall at night, Cave 329, the Early Tang Dynasty

Fetus Riding Elephant, Cave 329, the Early Tang Dynasty

Fetus Riding Elephant

Jiapiluowei was a state of very wealth in ancient India. King JingFan, a Shaikh of Sakya caste, was a valiant, able and saint-like person. He made the state prosperous and people peaceful after he came into the power. Young King JingFan, achieving his ambition at his early youth, being a Shaikh of Sakya caste and state head in politics, was the ideal lover in young princess and good-blooded girl's mind of various states. They dreamed to marry this promising youth, the King of Jiapiluowei state.

Moye, a little sister of Shanjue, the castellan of Tianbi town, was well-known for her neat and graceful look, decent manner and virtue. This pair of outstanding youth married creditably at last. They enjoyed their marriage happily year by year and with the passing of time, they became old unconsciously. A shading prevailed in their life because they had no a child to succeed to the throne. JingFan King was downhearted after returned from the work, his sensible wife understood him and gently advised him to escort other beautiful brides to his house so that one day he could have successor to the throne. JingFan King refused it and told his wife if he was destined to have no son, the result was the same whoever he married. He said it but his anxieties grew day by day. Moye, in a flash, was forty years old. One quiet night, she deeply slept in her bed, all of a sudden, an Deva, having a dignified appearance, riding a great white elephant, came into her dream, he came from the sky slowly and entered into her belly from the right side. She was awoken by this dream and told King JingFan being slept side of her. Both of them thought it mysterious. Moye lived leisurely same as before. She only liked skylarking or wandered about in secret woods or along lakeside.

Moye, not long after the dream, found that she was with a child, she told it to JingFan King. This good news, arising suddenly, excited and refreshed him, his torments and worries were cleared off. Ten months later, the prince was born under a Wuyou tree in DalanPini garden, Moye, in the course of childbearing, felt delighted. The new-born prince look around serenely. The legend goes that many miracles ever happened to him while the birth of prince as follows: nigh dragons perfumed his body; many Maharajas and Brahmadevas visited him, Maharaja-devass holed up four foot-posts of the colorfully glazed bed, Buddhist deities respectfully and cautiously opened a rare baldachin for him; numerous Devas appeared in the sky and gave out fragrant flowers. Sakyamuni stood on lotus after being born with one hand pointing at the sky and another one pointing to the earth, he said that he, from heaven and earth, was the number one, etc. The white elephant symbolized the propitiousness, Sakyamuni was the reincarnation of the white elephant.

Nails Hammered into King PeilenJie-li's Body

PeilenJie-li, the king of a state in ancient India with 84,000 villages under his jurisdiction, had 20,000 wives, maid-in-waiting, 500 prince as well as 10,000 ministers. He was kindhearted and looked upon common people as members of his own family. The king professed Buddhism and gave orders that whoever expounded Buddhist doctrine to him would be rewarded what he want. Raudraksa, a Brahmanist came to palace and said: "I know sutra, I can expound it to anybody if he likes." The king was overjoyed by his words, received him at the hall personally and prepared teaching room for him. Raudraksa said: "My Buddhist knowledge is accumulated in years of study, what will you pay me for it? " King replied: "You can get what you want, I spare no pains before you, master." Raudraksa said again: "I will hammer thousand nails into your body", the king promised him immediately, seven days later, Raudraksa would do it.

The king sent his men, 80,000 in number, to ride elephants to propagate it all over the state respectively.

Jataka of King Peilen Jie-li, the northern wall, Cave 275, the Northern Liang Dynasty

Both common people and officers gathered before the palace after hearing about it and persuaded the king: "We live and work in peace because of your merits and virtues, Please think about the interests of us, do not promise Raudraksa." The King's wives, maid-in-waiting as well as princes and ministers implored him: "Do not forsake the whole country and your life just for one Raudraksa." King PeilenJie-li thanked them for their love and esteem and said: " I, for all the living, ever killed numerous living beings in previous disasters, the piled bones of the dead will be higher than Xumi mountain; the collected bloodshed of the dead will be in excess of the water of five rivers; the tears of them gathered are greater than the seawater of four seas, but they were not the victims of Buddhism. I, only this time, will dedicate myself to Buddhism. I will stop your tears by use of the sapiential sword if I succeed. Why do you still stop me? "

The audients on hand listened to him quietly.

The king said to Raudraksa: "Your master, please expound Buddhist doctrine to me first, then do the nails, or else, I have no chance listen to sutra."

Raudraksa promised him in company with eulogistic words of "Nothing is immortal, miseries accompany all the living. No demiurge for world and world stands independently." Raudraksa finished his words and hammered thousand nails into King PeilenJie-li's body. All attendees kissed the ground and cried their hearts out, the world shook. All Devas were astonished and descended to the world to see what had happened in life. They could not control their tears while seeing that King PeilenJie-li dedicated himself to carrying forward Buddhist doctrine. Their heavy fall of tears became flowers all over the sky to attend King PeilenJie-li. Sakyamuni came to ask PeilenJie-li : "How brave you are ! What do you want for it? To be a Zhuanlun Wang ? Beelzebub or Indian King? " King answered: "No, just for Buddhism." Sakyamuni asked him again: "Regret? " King replied: " No, not at all" Sakyamuni asked: "Your proof? Show me, please ! " King PeilenJie-li vowed: "My nailed body will recover to prove me." King PeilenJie-li's body recovered before his words falling to the ground, all attendees were overjoyed.

King Moolight Dedicating His Head

Moolight, the king of a big and prosperous state in ancient India, had his court, being 40 miles in circumference, decorated with jewelries. He had numerous tribes, towns, wives, maid-in-waiting and treasures. His people lived and worked in peace. One day, an idea suddenly came into his mind that his whole nabobism had redounded upon the kindness and charity his preexistence paid. His future nabobism would be dashed into pieces if he stinted treasures this life. He decided to hand out his treasures to the poor for the sake of seeding the antecedents for his afterlife's nabobism. He called his ministers together and said to them: "I will, at the town gates and flourishing spots, hand out all my wealth to the common people. Please let all state know it." All monks, Brahmanists as well as the old, weak, orphan and widows came to receive treasures, foodstuffs and medicines handed out by King Moonlight. They sang the praise of King Moonlight, King Moonlight gained his fame.

PiMo-si, the king of a small and remote state in ancient India, heard of it and begrudged King Moonlight. He determined to make an end to King Moonlight so that he had chance to gain his fame similar to King Moonlight 's. He gave orders to call Taoists and able men all over the country together to look the way. All Brahmanists came in succession and were warmly feasted, in the meanwhile, they were told this ugly plan. They thought inwardly that King Moonlight's life was inalienable for his so kindhearted and honest merits and virtues. They, never more, helped a tyrant to do evil even if being punished. They retreated one after another and PiMo-si was angered at them. He ordered to offer a reward to look for able men and said: "Whoever brings King Moonlight's head will be rewarded the half of my country in company with my daughter." Raudrakasa, a non-Buddhist, lived in mountains, made response and claimed that he could meet PiMo-si. Seven days later, he set off together with what he needed.

King Moonlight Dedicating His Head, Cave 275, the Northern Liang Dynasty

The news related to Raudrakasa coming from long way to take Moonlight King's head incurred public wrath in and out side Xianshou town where the king lived. The door-god stopped Raudrakasa while he arrived at it. The Deity knew that King Moonlight liked to dedicate his all to those needed, he appeared in King Moonlight's dream and made a request: "You, well-beloved king, you show mercy on others and give those what they wanted, a beggar is outside your town, you should permit him to enter in." King Moonlight was startled to wake up. He ordered ministers to open town gate to all those wanted to enter in. Raudrakasa visited King Moonlight and said: "Little nabobism redounds upon the external things except for the body you handed out, boundless beneficence bases upon you body handed out! Nothing needed except for your head, Please grant me, my well-beloved King! "King Moonlight promised him without stint. It would come true seven days later. The kings of various states and common people implored Moonlight King in earnest words and with good intention and in the meanwhile exposed Raudrakasa's Jesuitism. King Moonlight refused them and said: "Attaining enlightenment, my long-cherished wish, I will rescue all of you out of the abyss of misery after I die for Buddhism, I will guide you to Pure Land, Do not stop me, Please! " They looked at each other and feel depressed. Raudrakasa, under a huge tree, chopped down King Moonlight's head. Whole people in the town together with ministers, grieved and indignation, cried their eyes out, all Devas were astonished and descended to the world. The sacred music suddenly burst over the sky.

King PiMo-si was overjoyed and jumped out of his skin while hearing the sacred music, then he felt startled and his heart broke and the Azrael shook hands with him. Raudrakasa took King Moonlight 's head out of the town. He could not bear the effluvial head while hearing news of King PiMo-si's death, he threw it and went away. He was cursed on his way and begged for nothing, he regretted what he had done. His heart suddenly broke and the hematemesis sent him to the Azrael.

Illustration of the Story of Nine Colored Deer, Cave 257, the Northern Wei Dynasty

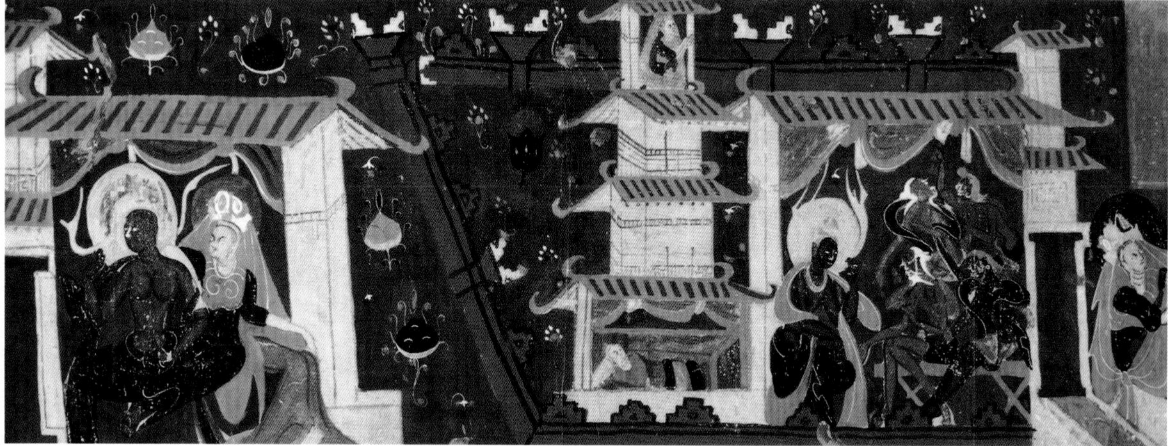

Nine-colored Deer's Story

Nine-colored deer was wandering along the Indian Ganges while the sound of voice "help", "help" coming into her ears from the river. She looked around and found a man falling into the river, and being rise and down along the roaring waves. He seemed to be engulfed by the waves. She, catching sight of it, jumped into the river regardless of her safety and saved him out after paying a lot of effort.

XuDa, just the man fallen into the river, frequently kowtowed to Nine-colored deer to requite her kindness though not yet being recovered from a fright. He said: "You, my savior, you have saven me, I swear to be your servant this life, protect you from damage and offer you water and grass whenever you need." The deer said: "Oh, No, Please, please go home, my poor XuDa! You are waited." XuDa hanged his head and continued his passionful words: "Oh, my savior, I'm conscious of a kindness and acknowledging a duty to repay it, Please, please give me a chance! " The deer was excited and firmly urged him to go home as soon as possible. She said: "Go home! Please, my dear Xuda, I only like to live alone, I can enjoy myself unfetteredly and I do not really like to abandon my free life for you! I will remember your kindness forever. Please do not expose my whereabouts to others! I hope." The deer urged him repeatedly, he vowed: "Please do

not worry, my savior, the tumefaction will cover my body and my mouth will emit effluvia if I break faith with you." He finished his words and set off.

The king doted upon his greedy and crafty queen for her charming gesture. One night, the Nine-colored deer appeared in the queen's dream, she told it to the king next morning that a nine-colored deer living within their territory, she would, after holding it, make a fur-padded mattress and antler-handled horsetail whisk which would match with her status as a queen. The king always followed queen's advice and gave orders over the country: "A reward of the half of the country together with a big silver bowl of golden beans as well as a big golden bowl of silver beans for catching the Nine-colored deer or exposing its whereabouts."

Xuda also heard this news. Nothing occupied his heart except for potential nabobism after revealing nine-colored deer's whereabouts. He reported it to warrior watched over the notice and then guided the king and his soldiers being good at toxophily to go to Ganges where the Nine-colored deer appeared and disappeared constantly. Ganges's tranquility was disordered by un-orderly and hurried clops. What lived in this field helped each other. Crow laid upon deer's head on the fly and told her what would happen to her as soon as he heard clops: "Hurry up, run away! They come to kill you." Unfortunately, the deer, though being willing, was still encircled by the king and his men. She was at swords' points and hung by a thread. She suddenly rushed at the king and said: "Wait a moment! Please, I have words for you before you kill me." The king said: "Please! " The Nine –colored deer told the king her story of saving Xuda out of the river and said her existence being beneficial to the country. The king was touched by her story and told her that it's Xuda to lead their way. The deer understood that Xuda she had rescued was real ungrateful, greedy and crafty. He, just for nabobism, peached against his savior. All attendees were affected by deer's narration. XuDa, being accused, felt too ashamed to show his face. He sweltered and could not say a word. At last, he came to end with the tumefaction covering his body and mouth emitting effluvia.

The king, herefrom, knew that the Nine-colored deer was a kindhearted mascot and gave orders over the country to strictly prohibit people catching and killing her, otherwise, the patriarchal clan would be involved in a criminal. The Nine-colored deer recovered her previous life along the Indian Ganges.

Jataka of Prince Sattva, Cave 428, the Northern Zhou Dynasty

Prince Sattva Sacrificing himself to Tigers

DaChe, the king of a state in ancient India, had three sons being named Mohe-Polo, Mohe-Tipo and Mohe-Sattva respectively.

One day, three princes went out for a tour together. They suddenly found seven new-born tigerlings cried piteously for food around their mother being dead-beat and at her last gasp. Three princes had a lot of sympathy with them. The elder prince said: "The death comes to them step by step, She, either to eat her children or to die together. It's terrible! Oh, my god!" The second prince said: "Yes.Too horrible to look at. What should we do for them?" They could do nothing about it except for nail-biting. The eye-catching sceneries along the way could not detain them. They were low in spirits and came back.

The eight life approaching death as well as brother's sorrowful and powerless expressions activated little prince Sattva. He went and meditated on it, the image of eight tiger's misery appeared in his mind constantly. "I have to save them, they ought enjoy themselves, I should sacrifice myself to those lived miserably, relieve them out of the abyss of misery!" Prince Sattva was refreshed and overjoyed after determining to sacrificing himself to feed tigers.

Sattva asked his brothers going first owing to being afraid of being discouraged. He came to tigers alone and lay by tiger's mouth nakedly. But to his disappointment that dead-beat tiger could do nothing. Sattva looked at the tigers vexedly and thought that his detainment would bring end to tigers. He would self-reproached

and covered the whole valley.

The tiger at her last gasp snuffled the blood and lapped which refreshed her appreciably, finally she ate up Sattva and went away together with her children. Sattva's brother returned to look for him after a long time's waiting. What came into their eyes were bloodily clothes and remains. They made out what left there were Sattva's. They regretted to leave their little brother alone and cried their hearts out.

The queen, in the meanwhile, was sleeping in the daytime. She suddenly dreamed about that her two breasts being sliced off together with her full teeth dropped as well as the little one of here three favorite pigeons was hold in glede's mouth. She woke up with a start and being told what had happened to her favorite son. She could not control here eyes and hurriedly came to the valley in company with the king. They were filled with deep sorrow and lost consciousness while finding Sattva's remains and clothes left for them. Finally, they were rescued to come to their senses and sent Sattva's remains back to palace as well as built a pagoda to attend Sattva's relics there. It enjoyed endless stream of pilgrims so that prince Sattva could attain enlightenment and become Buddha as soon as possible.

forever. He ascended up the cliff urgently and prayed silently for continuing tiger's lives. He then pierced his blood vessel by the aid of a dried bamboo and jumped down. A grand, solemn and stirring scene appeared in the world! All Devas were touched by him, sang praise of him. Numerous fragrant flowers descended down

Illustration of the Story of 500 Bandits Becoming Buddhas, Cave 285, the Western Wei Dynasty

Illustration of the Story of 500 Bandits Becoming Buddhas, Cave 285, the Western Wei Dynasty

Illustration of the Story of 500 Bandits Becoming Buddhas, Cave 285, the Western Wei Dynasty

500 Bandits become Buddhas

500 famished people of Sali state in ancient southern India rebelled. They occupied a mountain and based upon it to stand up to the government as an equal as well as plundered grains and repulsed government army's attacks time after time. The king was angered at written reports related to 500 bandits and sent able and vigorous troops to go on a punitive expedition.

The powerful government armies on imperial's order were well equipped. Their war-horses so much as were put on armors and to be invulnerability. As for 500 bandits, just the other way, they looked interior in strengthen by comparison and all had been captured in this unheard-of fierce battle because of being outnumbered.

The feudal official abominated these bandits who did not bow down to obey submissively and executed their exoculation owing to their flagrances and in the meanwhile to give a lesson to others.

On that day, the execution ground was alert strictly and hellishly. 500 bandits were sent to the execution ground under escort along with the orders given by supervisor sat in higher position imperially. They were half naked, hair- disheveled, and black and blue. Executioners were devil-like. The terror-stricken attendees were too horrible to look at the bloody execution. 500 bandits became blind men several hours later and were exiled in desolate and uninhabited mountains far from towns and villages. They had nothing except for being companied by wild animals. They could not control themselves despairingly, ran and jumped hysterically, squalled grievously.

Sakyamuni heard this sound of voice and understood what had happened to 500 bandits. He, by right of his extraordinary power, sent wonder drugs with strong aroma into their eyes. Instantly, their eyes got well and the rebirth came to them. Surprised bandits understood that Sakyamuni had rescued them while Sakyamuni standing before them. They prostrated themselves before Sakyamuni to thank for his kindness and accept his edification. Sakyamuni said to them at leisure: "Numerous predestined fates are waiting for all earthlings. Whoever hides his wrongdoing and praises his good deeds will be freed from the abyss of misery and guided to Pure Land, the punishment or reward will be distributed in a future life based on performance in this one. You are punished because you went against your superiors and insurrection. You will enjoy endless happiness if you thoroughly reform yourselves and convert to Buddhism from now on."

All of them kissed the ground to show repentance after being edified and respected Sakyamuni their master. They converted themselves to Buddhism and were initiated into monk-hood by Sakyamuni personally. They studied Buddhism with great concentration, they, many years later, had succeeded in attaining enlightenment in the end.

Jataka of King Sivi, Cave 254, the Northern Wei Dynasty

King Sivi's Bartering Body for Pigeon

Sivi, the beneficent king of a big state of wealth in ancient India, made Tipodi the capital of his state. He treated common people as members of his own family and extended policies of benevolence. He commanded 84, 000 small states; had 20, 000wives, maid-in-waiting as well as 500 princes and as many as 10,000 ministers. His people lived and worked in peace.

Dishi, the Maharaja-devas of the 33rd layer of the sky, had a foreboding that his death would come. Stewed Dishi told it to his close minister PiShou-tian while he asked. Dishi said: "I'm going to die, but the worldly power of Buddha has disappeared, all great Bodhisattvas couldn't be seen anymore, I'm troubled, what should I do? " PiShou-tian said: "Ask for Sivi, a king in the land of the living, he aspires to attain enlightenment." Dishi half believed and half doubted, he determined to test Sivi himself. He asked PiShou-tian to become a pigeon and himself an eagle gone after the pigeon.

The eagle followed after the pigeon who flying to the king Sivi and hidden under his oxter for help. The eagle couldn't catch it and said to the king Sivi: "I'm hungry to die, Please return my pigeon, please! " The king Sivi said: " No, I have ever sworn to release all the living from sufferings, so I'm sorry, I can't return this pitiful pigeon." The eagle said again: "Your respectful King, you love all the living, include me, Ok? I'm hungry to die if you refuse me." The king Sivi said after thought : "Would you like meat? " The eagle replied: "Off course, but only refresh meat." The king Sivi thought within himself: "I couldn't sacrifice this one to save another one, Nothing can save two both of them except for my body." He ordered his servant to fetch a knife and sliced a piece of meat off his leg for the eagle. But the eagle said: "Your respectful king, you are almsgiver, you like to barter your meat for this pigeon, Ok! Please weigh meat out as many as that of the pigeon." The steelyard was brought. To his astonishment that the total weight of his leg meat sliced together with that sliced from his whole body actually was less than that of this pigeon. The king Sivi determined to sacrifice himself to save this pigeon though he felt puzzled. He tried to sit on scale pan but failed and lost his consciousness. He tried again very reluctantly and succeeded this time after he came to himself. They were well matched in weight. The heaven palace was trembled, all Devas appeared in the sky and sang praise of him, they couldn't control their tears. Then they gave out numerous flowers to attend him. Dishi showed his colors and said to the king Sivi: "Your have boundless beneficence, you are capable of being the ruler of the world. What do you want? " The king said: "Nothing but to carry forward Buddhist doctrine." Dishi asked again: "Now, you see, your wound is still paining, do you regret it? " The king replied: "No regrets, not at all! " Dishi said: "No regrets? Look at your agonizing expression, How can I believe you? " The king Sivi vowed: "I have never regretted what I did, my limbs and trunk will recover if my wish of becoming Buddha is true and realized". To all attendee's excitement that the king's body was recovered as expected after his oaths. Both heaven and the world were overjoyed, highly praised him and danced rapturously.

Beggar Becoming Rich

A moneybags lived in a small town in ancient India. He ever had a lovely boy who had lost his way while plaid outside at his age of about 7. This boy latterly lived a vagrant life in foreign states and became a beggar with Qiongzi as his name. With ages, Qiongzi came back his birthplace at his 40years of age unconsciously. On day, he begged for food before a moneybags' door. He looked up, to his astonishment that what appeared in his eyes were magnificent houses arranged in rows just as the towering and sacred imperial palace. He laughed in his sleeve that it's not the place for a beggar to visit. He couldn't stay here any longer, he, suddenly, found a old man who wearing magnificent clothes was looking at him while he looking back. "It is the king! ". He thought and ran away hurriedly because of the dread.

This old man was a moneybags who had ever lost his only son and failed in searching him out. He was cheerless all days because he had no child to succeed to his countless wealth in the future. He became conscious of that this beggar being very similar to his lost son in the appearance and age. He hurriedly sent servants to bring the beggar to him. The pitiful beggar suddenly lost his consciousness before the moneybags owing to suffering hunger and dread. The moneybags carefully studied his appearance and firmly believed that the beggar was just his son he was looking for.

The old man showed tender care for him spontaneously. He, half grieved and half pleased, was delighted and concealed this news from others. The beggar, being provided with necessities in life, was concerned about in everyway by the moneybags. He, unavoidably, felt puzzled and dread. He bid farewell to moneybags and continued his vagabond life. The moneybags was sentimental at his son's leave because they just now reunited by chance. He, out of concern for his safety and living, sent a servant to look for and bring him back. The beggar was found and engaged to clear away the dejecta at the moneybags family. He asked to be paid in advance for being afraid of being cheated, the moneybags promised him readily. The beggar, from now on, ended his vagabond life and diligently worked for the moneybags. Looking at his emaciated stature, haggard face and shabby clothes, moneybags' pity on him cropped up spontaneously. The moneybags took off his magnificent clothes instead of work clothes and came to the scene where the beggar was working and said to him: "You are a vagrant, I'm a single old man, I'll pay you double wages, provide with you what you need and treat you as my son if you don't mind working here for long term, Ok? " The beggar thought with himself that he turned up trumps to meet such a kindhearted and genial old man. He began to regard himself one member of this family and treat the old man as his father. He took part in the management of daily works on his own initiative besides working hard. The moneybags was released from worries and enjoyed himself every day.

One day, the moneybags was beset with sickness and he understood that his end was coming. He summoned the beggar and said to him: "Now, you know the quantity of my warehouses and treasures within them. I always look upon you as my son, and you do me your father, I'm going to leave you all my wealth when I pass away. I hope you can keep them! " The beggar was so overjoyed at it that a he couldn't believe himself. He thought he was in daydream. He treated the old man as his relative respectfully and considered him with deep solicitude. As for treasures and other works, he didn't make any arbitrary decisions prior to soliciting for the moneybags' consent, he still lived in house prepared for hired labors, he looked himself and showed little pride and prejudice before others.

The moneybags' condition, before long, became worse, all his relatives and friends were invited. He declared in public: "This beggar is just my son lost fifty years ago. I have left him all my wealth. All you here, please, testify on behalf of him, please! ". All attendees were pleased at this news and congratulated them on their reunion.

Beggar Becoming the Rich, Cave 85, the Late Tang Dynasty

Story of Bhiksuni Patacara, Cave 296, the Northern Zhou Dynasty

Bhiksuni Patacara

Patacara, born in a family of wealth in ancient India, one day, carried her little son in her arms and led her elder one to go her mother's home. Unfortunately, a river with turbulent waves blocked their way. She was in a dilemma, several minutes later, an idea came into her minds. She told her elder son: "My poppet, stay here, don't move! I will take your brother to opposite bank first, then I come back to receive you, Ok? " Her elder son promised her and she crossed the river and put her little son on the grassland nearby the river. Just at this moment, an accident happened, her elder son delightfully walked down the bank to receive his mother and was taken away by the violent waves while she returned. She tried her best to look for him but he failed, she stood in river unconsciously and did not know how long she was there. Suddenly, she came to earth and remembered her little son. She rushed to look for him in grassland, but to her disappointment, only bloodstains and her little son's remains were found, wild wolves had eaten up her child. She grieved to the extent of wishing to die and struggled to go her mother's home.

Her mother understood and considered her distressful daughter in every way. Patacara gradually refreshed herself. A Brahmanic young man, being addicted to drink, was fascinated with her good looks and married her. One day, she was delivering her child while her tipsy husband knocked at the door. She couldn't get up to open the door for him. As a result, her angered husband broke into the house, grasped her hair and gave her a good beating though she explained. Her tipsy husband was atrocious, he sliced the new-born child into pieces and fried them. She was enforced to eat her child, how terrible it was for her! She struggled to refuse him but she failed. She had to eat them because of being whipped.

Disappointed Patacara discarded her family and lived a vagabond life owing to her conscienceless husband. She, in Brahnai state, encountered a young man of wealth, who was attracted by her good looks, he had a lot of sympathy with Patacara while being told what had happened to her. They looked after each other and finally they were in love and married. But good times didn't last long, her husband died of incurable disease. She was buried with the dead according to local custom of the day that the dead' favorite wife and others during his life should be buried together with him. The rich funerary objects attracted robbers, as result, she was saved and was enforced to marry the head of robbers. The head of robbers, before long, was captured and beheaded by feudal official. His remnants stole the corpse and delivered it to Patacara, this time she was buried with the dead again. Three days later, wild wolves dug the grave, ate up the corpse and tore her clothes into pieces only. She was still alive. She struggled to get out the grave and stood in wind as naked as when she was born. She thought deeply why she was so unfairly and continuously treated in the land of living, where their end was. She went towards the wilds with her hair dishevelled.

Patacara, from this time on, understood thoroughly the all existed in world. She desired nothing, entered into Buddhism and became a Bhiksuni.

Meditating Bodhisattva, Cave 71, the Early Tang Dynasty

Buddha, Cave 328, the High Tang Dynasty

Avalokitesvara on the North Side of the Central Niche, Cave 328, the Early Tang Dynasty

Buddha in Dhyana, Cave 259, the Northern Wei Dynasty

Bodhisattva, Cave 196, the Late Tang Dynasty

Great Buddha, Cave 130, the High Tang Dynasty

Donors

Both dedicating personal belongs and being attendants constitute the concept of the donor. Male and female people who gave alms to temple and made greater contributions to Buddhist master are called donors. The former are called alms giver, the later the attendants.

The figures of donors can be seen in most grottoes in Mogao Grotto. They, in company with Mogao Grotto, have experienced over 1000 years of development. They are tied with Buddhist existence and development closely. Their important role goes without saying. Donors' identities marked in Mogao Grotto' murals are diversified as follows: monks, nuns, male attendants, female attendants, higher officials and nobles, common people, soldiers, merchants, slaves and maids, etc. As for grottoes excavated by donors, they are also diversified as follows: being excavated by a monk group alone; being co-excavated by many monk groups; being done by a official family alone as well as being done by populace communities jointly. In a word, they excavated grottoes according to their abilities and took flexible manners. The donors would inscribe their names and figures on well-marked places within a grotto when they came to a successful end.

Female Donors, Cave 225, the Early Tang Dynasty

Female Donors, Cave 329, the Early Tang Dynasty

What's the purpose of a donor who did it at all costs? The following inscriptions extracted will answer it. As stated in the inscription in Cave 160: " Buddha's kindness releases souls from purgatory. I am ZhangJin-tong, being clear and upright, the former officer in charge of offering amnesty and enlistment to rebels in Hexi region. I believe in Buddhism. I dedicate my belongs to mold a Buddha's figure and those of his two disciples in company with a illustration of thousand Buddha and two Flying Devi. What I want is to have a successful end." In Cave 335, the inscription on upper corner north of the eastern wall's door said: "We believe in Buddhism, being free from care, we, together with our family, did it in May 17 to wish the soul of the dead to go Pure Land, those in life to enjoy themselves." Excavating grottoes to pray blessings for the dead and those in life are basic purposes besides delivering long-cherished wishes. For instance, the monk or nun hopes to attain enlightenment; the official families wish to be rich, keeping ranks and enjoying happiness for generations. They all gave priority to expiate the sins of the dead though having different wishes themselves.

The full-bodied Buddhist culture is influenced greatly by traditional Chinese ethic and morality. The size of donors' figures in grottoes is inversely proportional to the grotto's excavation time. Small size, as small as 10-odd cm tall in donors' figures painted in grottoes being excavated before Sui Dynasty; large size, as big as life, in donors' figures painted in grottoes being excavated since the Five Dynasties. The two donors' figures in Cave 225 and Cave 329, the magnum opus of donors' figures, were painted true to life, kindly and amiably. They, in stains and positions, differ from those being painted similarly in another grottoes. They are organically merged into the Buddhist art.

Attendant Bodhisattva, Cave 401, the Early Tang Dynasty

A Musician Playing Piga with Her Hands Behind Her Back, Cave 112, the Mid-Tang Dynasty

Celestial Performer

Both the singer and dancer were generally called "dancer" in ancient time, but those being adept at playing various musical instruments were called "musician". In big illustrations of sutra in Mogao Grotto, especially in those of Pure Land sutra and Buddha's expounding Buddhist doctrine, dancers and musicians can be seen everywhere. They are called celestial performers. The Vol.10 of "Sastra on the Prajna-paramita sutra" says that Grandharva had ever been the performer of Devas. Celestial performer's the graceful image, simple and naive looks are very interesting. The figure of a musician playing the lute with her hands behind her back being painted in Cave112 becomes the symbol of Dunhung city nowadays who welcoming all visitors from all directions. The more than 3400 figures of celestial performers, figures of 490 bands in large or small scale, as well as 4300 musical instruments of 44 different kinds can be seen in total 200-odd grottoes. They enrich Buddhist art, play music while doing Buddhist ceremony and make Pure Land sacred. The title and image of celestial performers are diversified. They change along with the murals' content and actual situations. For example, those Devas, Bodhisattvas and Flying Devi being engaged on dancing and played music, are called heaven palace's performers in Pure Land depicted in illustration of Pure Land sutra; those Yaocha played musical instruments under the lower part of murals or around the rite are called Yaocha performers; in the illustration of Buddha's expounding Buddhist doctrine, those flew around, disseminated aromatic flowers and played musical instruments are called Flying Devi performers; those boys, cropped up from lotus, carried musical instruments in arms and played are called flower-born performers; those Bodhisattvas in rows carried musical instruments in arms and played are called Bodhisattva's performers; those appeared in the illustration of Amitabha sutra, man-headed and bird-bodied, crane-shaped with spread wings, wore Bodhisattva's crown as well as carried musical instruments in arms and sang happily in a loud voice are called Jialin Pinjia performers. The varieties of the musical instrument are diversified as follows: lute, harp, Fangxiang, flute, Paixiao, zither, qin, clappers, Stradivarius, drum, sheng and Ruanxian, etc. These diversified musical instruments not only make the Pure Land sacred but also reflect the situation of peace and prosperity of those days true to life.

Musicians of Offerings, a Mural Depicts Celestial Chinese Wind Pipe, Lute and Clipper Players, Cave 159, the Mid-Tang Dynasty

They descended from the heaven and merged into common people's daily life and to be appreciated by them. The musical instruments carried by donor's performers; employed in the outgoing, marriage and feast are similar to those played by celestial performers in Pure Land. Dunhuang Academy, after cooperation with organizations concerned, has reproduced the most of musical instruments appeared in Dunhuang's murals and held a large-scale concert to play them during the International Academic Proseminar hold at Nine-Storied Square in Mogao Grotto in August of 2004. It's the great event for ancient musical instruments to descend from grottoes to real life and people were lucky to respectfully appreciate the verve given by them.

Dancer and Musicians, Cave 112, the Mid-Tang Dynasty

Dancers and Musicians, the Northern Wall, Cave 220, the Early Tang Dynasty

Thirteen Musicians in a Mural Have Different Skin Colors. This is a Scenene of Court Entertainment, Cave 220, the Early Tang Dynasty

Mural of Bodhisattas of Offerings Show Painting Styles of Central China and Western Countries, Cave 285, the Western Wei Dynasty

Mural of Bodhisattvas of Offerings Show Painting Styles of Central China and Western Countries, Cave 285, the Western Wei Dynasty

Dual Dance, a Mural Depicts Two Dancers Dancing on a Small Piece of Carpet, Scholars Think this is a Dance from the Western Regions, Cave 220, the Early Tang Dynasty

Slaughter house, Cave 85, the Late Tang Dynasty

Battle Scene of the Illustration of the Saddharma pundarika Sutra, the Southern Wall, Cave 12, the Late Tang Dynasty

Flying Devi on the Ceiling, Cave 329, the Early Tang Dynasty

Lotus Square Ceiling with Three Rabbits, Cave 407, the Sui Dynasty

Groom Taming Horse, Cave 288, the Western Wei Dynasty

Groom and His Horse, Cave 290, the Northern Zhou Dynasty

Wild Ox, Cave 249, the Western Wei Dynasty

Hunting Detail, Features Simple and Flowing Lines, Cave 249, the Western Wei Dynasty

Dunhuang Calligraphy

More than ten thousand writings or paintings of the Jin, Sixteen States, Sui, Tang and Northern Song Dynasties collected in Dunhuang literature are regarded as the most complete, systematic and the first-hand material to study the evolvement and development of Chinese regular script and calligraphic art respectively. The Dunhuang literature's chirography changed with the passage of time. The font style of them would expose the time they were finished, it will help people to study Dunhuang literature significatively. The full-bodied religious tint and the trait relating to humankind lived in north-west China characterize the Dunhuang literature's font style because of the religious requirement and specifically historical situation of Dunhuang region. Dunhuang literature's font style of near 1000 years history, for these reason, is named "Sutra's Style" which come from the common labor of sutras copiers in past dynasties. The most of sutra copiers were common people and nameless. They did it to make a living. Their prominent calligraphy and names were not recoded in history and literature concerned owing to their lower position of status in the community. Their names, once in a while, can be found there just for the purposes of seeing about the scribal quality. "Sutra's Style" was evolved from the calligraphy of "Inscribed bamboo slips" of Han Dynasty and the base of the regular script of both Sui and Tang Dynasties. It not only recorded the overall process of Chinese characters evolving from official script to standard script but also contributed to the progress of Chinese characters. "Sutra's Style", the main chirography for copying sutras since the Jin Dynasty, has a certain formula and limit. Firstly, to sketch out the checks and columns on papers concerned; secondly, to write down the sutra name, illustration name at the top row of the volume header, then to transcribe sutra at another row, finally to write down the sutra's order and vows, etc. The number of rows and words in a piece of paper were limited certainly. To be font specification and self-absorption during the transcription were regarded as respecting Buddha. "Sutra's Style", the script, prevailed in those days. Numerous characters in popular form can be found in transcribed sutras owing to copiers' lower status in those days so that the folk decorative style had been merged into the font style unavoidably. It's the beneficial apocalypse for us to understand the origination of the simplified character.

The changes in font evolved from official script to regular script and that in applying the brush pen were obvious since the Han Dynasty. The chaos caused by wars taken place during the period of the Jin Dynasty and that of both the Southern and Northern Dynasties slowed down the progress of Chinese characters, as a result, the words in Dunhuang literature were the compound of both official script and regular script during this period. Being very thin at the start of each stroke in writing, being thick and round at the end stroke in writing as well as polliwog-shaped characterized it together. As for a word with many strokes, it looked just as polliwogs got together from all directions. It's the complex of Han calligraphy's stagnant and energetic style and that of both the Wei and Jin's rigid pen. The rigid pen, a dip pen made of metal, bone, bamboo or wood in those days, could be applied to write directly. Easy operation, thin and weak font, little artistic and aesthetic quality characterized it together. The official script in both the Qin and Han Dynasties, the compound of both the official and regular script in the Wei, Jin, both Southern and northern Dynasties as well the regular script since the Sui and Tang Dynasties constituted the progress stage of "Sutra's Style". As for every stage, the font style in early moment differed with that in later. They, even now, interacted closely and sometimes interlaced.

Sutra Written in Western Xia Words

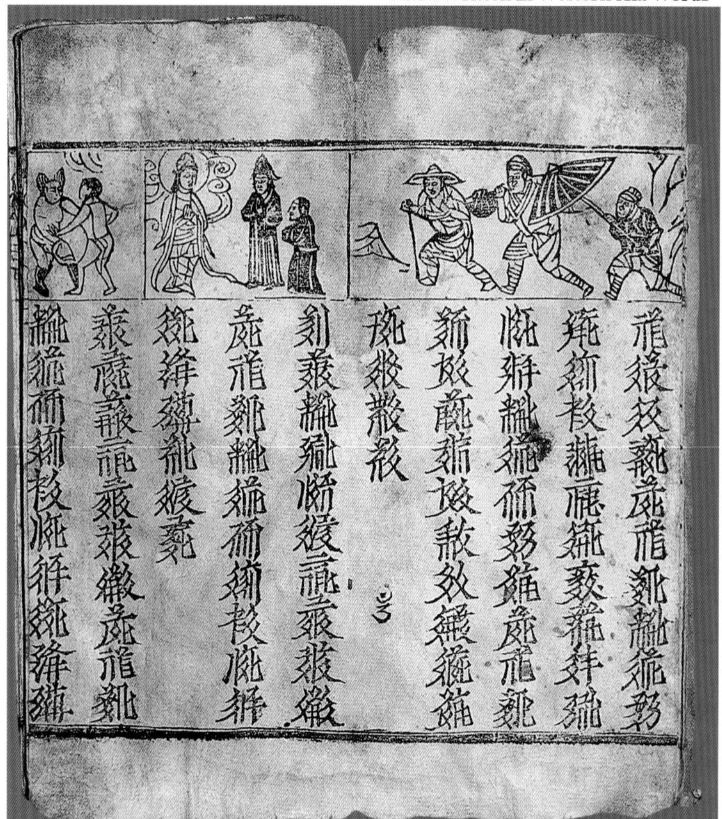

Inscribed Bamboo Slips unearthed at Dunhuang

"Jian", the bamboo slips for writing on in brush pen during the period from the Warring States Period to the Wei and Jin Dynasties. The wooden tablets or slips, being called "Zha" or "Du", together with the bamboo slips were called "Jian" generally. Many series-wound slips were called "Ce" (volume). The inscribed bamboo slips are rare material for researching ancient Chinese history.

The most of total 1217 "Jian" unearthed at the beacon fire's site in Dunhuang's Maquanwan are wooden slips owing to being without bamboo produced in ancient Dunhuang region. They indicate that the original Han's Yumen Pass was set up in the west side of the beacon fire's site in Dunhuang's Maquanwan nowadays, not Xiaofangpan town. As recorded in a slip (a wattle recorded the beacon tower's set-up in Yumen Pass) that Shili(an ancient official title)commanded five soldiers, Houzhang(an ancient official title) the seven soldiers, Houli(an ancient official title) the eight soldiers as well as the head of beacon group commanded twenty-nine soldiers and three soldiers under the jurisdiction of Houlingli(an ancient official title). It shows that beacon fire's site in Maquanwan was under jurisdiction of Hou official and to be the place where Hou official stationed, too. The beacon fire's site unearthed at Maquanwan, for the first time, helps people understand not only the relations between Douwei, Houzhan, Houli, Houguan, Suizhang and town, Zhang, Wu and Sui in Dunhuang region but also the scale, layout, structure, building way and function of counterguard, beacon towers and fertile farmland of the Han Dynasty.

70years has past since Han's inscribed bamboo slips being unearthed at Dunhuang. The international academia replies to it greatly. The numerous textual research and explains are carried out by scholars both at home and abroad. In March of 1981, 4 Han's inscribed bamboo slips were discovered by farmers at the beacon fire's site in the north of Xihu in Danghe village, Dunhuang city. The workers of city's cultural center collected another 70-odd wooden slips there. The azimuth of this beacon fire's site is D380, namely the position is longitude94°08′east and latitude 40°27′north. The aerial pictures show that it's the cone-shaped mesa eroded by wind. What being inscribed on wooden slips, being made of local diversiform-leaved poplar and Chinese tamarisk, touched upon the imperial orders, laws and decrees, an official call to arms, daily books for keeping accounts related to the garrison troops, transcription, almanac, letters and others. They were made in the 7th year of Shiyuan of the Emperor Han Zhaodi's reign in the Western Han Dynasty (i.e. A.D. 80), and being found for the first time in China. They indicate that the Emperor Wu of the Han Dynasty had ever given orders to set up four prefectures and two passes in Dunhuang region to solidify the frontier defence. Dunhuang, known as the throat of ancient Silk-road, was celebrated for relying against Qilian Mountains in the south, bordering on the Western Lands in the west, being encircled by Minsha Mountain and accompanied by Dang River, both Yang Pass and Yumen Pass situated in its south and north respectively, controlling Yixi region and leading the way to Mobei. 150km of the Han's Great Wall together with its 70-odd beacon towers are kept in actual existence within Dunhuang region.

They, just as forbidding barriers, safeguard the door to the western frontier. What being inscribed on numerous Han's inscribed bamboo slips reflect the Dunhuang region's social life of the time. Dunhuang, the representative of important frontier towns, stood in the front line of northwestern frontier of those days, its geographical situation naturally slowed down the business prosperity because of large numbers of soldiers being stationed at this region with the native-born population of 20,000 in number. They influenced the local economic advance greatly. The numerous Han's inscribed bamboo slips unearthed at Dunhuang expose the details of the military affairs, farming, business and handicraft industry of the day in this region, they will redound to the farther discussion of the ancient frontier phylogeny.

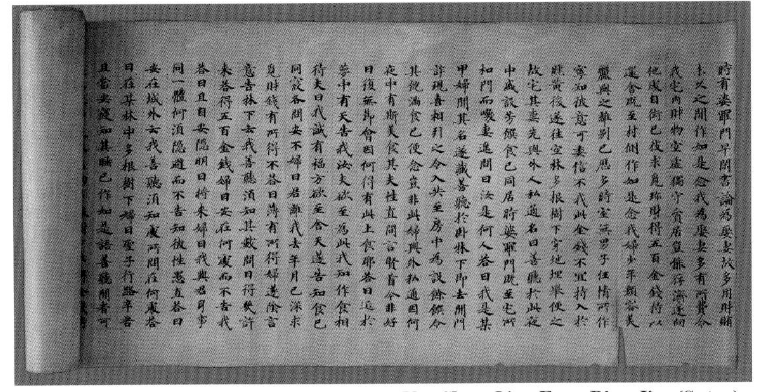

Buddha's Utterance of Da Yao Shan Qiao Fang Bian Jing(Sutra)

Inscribed Bamboo Slips Dating Back to the Han Dynasty Unearthed in Dunhuang

Yulin Grotto

Yulin Grotto, alias Wanfo Gorge, lies in a valley 75km to southwest Anxi County. Anxi County lies at the western end of Hexi Corridor and ever to be an important town on the Silk-road as well as a key center for the exchange of economy, culture, politic, diplomacy between central plains and the foreign countries of the day. In the Spring and Autumn Period, Anxi County was called Guazhou where Darouzhi people once lived and the Hunnish Hunye Headman once had it under his jurisdiction. It was the popedom of Dunhuang Prefecture in the Han Dynasty and divided into Guazhou and Shazhou in the period of Wude of the Tang Dynasty, of which, Anxi County was called Guazhou and Dunhuang was called Shazhou. The Song Dynasty called it Guazhou and the Ming Dynasty set Handongwei (i.e. title of official office) to manage it as well as the Qing Dynasty set Anxi Zhilizhou (i.e. administerial area). Finally, the Public of China (1919-1949) named it Anxi County in 1913. In the Han and the Jin Dynasties, large quantities of persons had been immigrated together with advanced techniques and culture of the central plains. The productive forces and the culture there accordingly had been improved greatly, in the meanwhile, the ruling class of the day energetically pubilicized Buddhism there, aforementioned action promoted the development of the Buddhism and resulted in the excavation of Buddhist grottoes.

Yulin Grotto is one of famous grottoes in China and an important part of the Dunhuang art as well. It was excavated on both sides of the valley in the Northern Dynasty with 43 caves in total being in actual existence together with statures and murals of the Tang Dynasty, the Five Dynasties, the Song Dynasty, the Western Xia regime, the Yuan Dynasty and the Qing Dynasty as well as the Republic of China (1919-1949). Of which, 32 caves are on the eastern cliff and 11 caves on the western cliff of the valley. The space between them is 100-odd meters with Yulin River runs away in front of them. The existing caves tell that Yulin Grotto had ever been repaired and amended on a large scale before the Tang Dynasty. The original appearance of Yulin Grotto can't be seen owing to the changes of times, the destruction of human being and the nature and many times of maintenance to it by generations. Yulin Grotto enjoys high Buddhist art value, especially its caves and murals of the Western Xia regime and the Yuan Dynasty, they supply a gap of no cave ever being excavated in Mogao Grotto in the times of the Western Xia regime.

The "central stupa-shaped pillar", "the vault

The Appearance of the Yulin Grottoes

top" and "truncated pyramid ceiling" characterize the shape and structure of Yulin Grotto. Cave 17, Cave 28 and Cave 39 pertain to "central stupa-shaped pillar", i.e. the shape and structure of early caves in Yulin Grotto where the original murals had been covered by later ones. The Cave 3 and Cave 6 pertain to the type of "vault top" where the Buddha altar being built. The esoteric Tibetan Buddhism made much impact on the caves of the Yuan Dynasty, the central Buddha altar became rounded or octagon in shape in that time with exception of the square caves there being the same as that of the Tang and Song Dynasties.

The Tang Dynasty was a period of great prosperity in ancient China and for Yulin Grotto of the day. Not only the specification and quantities but also the artistic value of the caves excavated in that period are unparalleled in history. Cave 25 is a representative of them. In the period of the Five Dynasties and the Song Dynasty, Cao family dominated Guazhou and Shazhou, they established friendly relationship with both Huihu headman and Yutian King by the marriage. It resulted in excavating caves and building imperial art academy on a large scale owing to the steady and prosperous environment in both Guazhou and Shazhou. Cave 35 is a representative of the day. The caves excavated in the Western Xia regime and the Yuan Dynasty added new contents, for example the figure of Kuan-yin gazing at the moon in the water, to the grotto art. Both Cave 3 and Cave 4 are representatives of them. Speak of the murals' contents and their style, Yulin Grotto and Mogao Grotto had many affinities except for their respective features in the style. Yulin Grotto, the achievement of ancient Chinese, was designated the one of the first group of the key cultural relics protected by country in 1961.

Samantabhadra, Southern Part of the Western Wall, Cave 3, the Western Xia Dynasty

Manjusri and His Suite, Northern Part of the Western Wall, Main Chamber, Cave 25, the Tang Dynasty

Illustration of Maitreya Sutra

Illustration of Maitreya Sutra in Cave 25 of Dunhuang's Yulin Grotto was painted in the Tibetan times. As for the murals in Dunhuang, 95 murals are Illustration of Maitreya Sutra. Colorful composition of a picture, clear line, lively figures and rich contents characterize the theme of the illustration of the Pure Land, alias the illustration of Maitreya Pure Land. The Illustration of Maitreya sutra, based upon Budhha's superior stage of the Tusita prince, was painted independently in the Sui Dynasty at earliest. These illustrations painted from the Early Tang Dynasty to the Song Dynasty are different from the previous in the composition of a picture. They combined content of Idem into the same mural, the Buddha's supeior stage was depicted in the upper position of it and the Idem in the lower position of it. The illustration of the Maitreya Sutra depicts many Buddhist stories, 20-odd in total as follows: the birth of Maitreya, a lotus flowers from seven steps, an aged man entering into the grave, sowing one and harvesting seven, Naga-puspa sending robe as well as becoming Buddha under the Naga-puspa, etc, each details is vivid. Logical composition of a picture, strewn at random as well as vivid depiction and layout in good order together characterize them. Visitors will have sense of beauty of Buddhist art while they viewing them.

Maitreya, alias "Mile" in China, means Benevolent. As sated in sutra that Maitreya born in a Brahmin family became a disciple of Buddha and died earlier than Buddha did. Maitreya, a vegetarian, expounds Buddhist truth to Devas in name of Bodhisattva, lives in the heaven palace of the Tusita prince and blesses the human. Maitreya, from those of the Buddha clan, gives priority to kindness of Buddha's kindness, pity, joy and humility, and continues the worldly seed of Buddhahood, accordingly is called Benevolent or Benevolent-Bodhisattva. The sutra also said that Sakyamuni once predicted that Maitreya would become Buddha under Naga-puspa while he being 4000 years-old (i.e. 5.76 billion years in the world), then make three groups in the diamond-realm, expound Buddhist truth to the early beings in stead of him. Maitreya accordingly is called the Eka-jati-prati-baddha or the Future Buddha. Maitreya-

Scene of a Man on His Death Bed, Detail of the Illustration of the Maitreya Sutra, Northern Wall, Main Chamber, Cave 25, The Tang Dynasty.

bodhisattva, till then, would achieve all wisdom of Sakyamuni and become Buddha, and be called Maitreya-Buddha or Maitreya-Tathagata. Many scenes related to the real life cab be seen in the illustration of Maitreya, such as plowing, sowing, harvesting, threshing gain, loading grain into granary, etc. They truly reflect the agricultural procedures and the life of the day, include the farm tools, such as plough (farmers call it "two cows plowing"), bending plough, reaping hook, chariot driven by cow, shackles, besom made of grass, the fork of six sections made of Chinese tamarisk branches, etc. These tools still can be seen in Dunhuang rural area.

The Idem says that person would enter into the tomb while his hour comes, who come to the mountain forest to rest himself and then to be nirvana before Mahabrahman and all the Devas while he nearing his end. The mural depicts that an aged man, holding a stick is his hand, went to his tomb with the help of his offspring, some attendants followed him with his clothes in hands; the other murals depict that an aged man with white hairs and moustaches sat in a round tomb, one boy kissed the ground to bid adieu to him with other family numbers and attendants standing on both sides of the tomb or weeping. The ancient painters hoped to present the spirit of doing not seek the fame and wealth in life, enjoying the ease and serenity as well as hoping to go the Pure Land as early as possible while his end coming.

Ploughing and Harvesting,the North Wall, Cave 25 of the Yulin Grottoes, The Mid-Tang Dynasty

The Illustration of Maitreya Sutra takes open and free composition, all acts of human living and Devas are depicted in natural conditions. Maitreya expounding Budda's doctrines in the Buddha's woods is the focus of it, then other various beautiful events are showed, such as the continuous mountains, the streams, the boundless universe, Kassapa revealing his theurgies, Devas flying towards the heaven paradise by rosy clouds, the theme of the mural thus can be made to stand out. All subject matters painted in the illustration of Maitreya Sutra reflects the real life of the human being, which shows that Devas life in Maitreya's world was not divorced from the real life and natural rule. They only try to change the world and make it the real pure land by their celestial power.

Musicians and Dancers, Cave 15 of the Yulin Grottoes.The Mid-Tang Dynasty.

Musicians and Dancers, Cave 15 of the Yulin Grottoes. The Mid-Tang Dynasty

Buildings on the Southern Wall, the Yulin Grottoes, Cave 25, The Mid-Tang Dynasty

Western Thousand Buddha Grotto

Western Thousand Buddha Grotto

Western Thousand Buddha Grotto lies 35 km to southwest Dunhuang city. As stated in Shazhou geography which pertained to the Dunhuang documents being compiled by Tang government and preserved in Paris nowadays that Western Thousand Buddha Grotto situated at a spot 60 Li to the east Youzai county (i.e. Shouchang county), and its first grotto was excavated by a official and then more and more people excavated others one after another. The Western Thousand Buddha Grotto just came of it. For this cause, as to the date of its excavation, it's e Western earlier than that of Mogao Grotto or both of them shared the same times at the latest. Its scale might exceed or equal to that of Mogo Grotto. Only 22 caves are in actual existence because of natural and man-made disaster. Firstly, it's excavated on cliff beside the Danhe River, the water level of the day was higher, the quick water stroke this Yumen arenaceous cliff. Secondly, the loose and big gravels were easily airslaked. They resulted in the damage of Western Thousand Buddha Grotto during past years. The most of these 22 caves were also damaged more or less, say nothing of comparing their dimensions and contents with Mogo Grotto's. No clear records within them can tell us the time of their excavation except for the style of the construction, statues and murals there. It's initially excavated in the beginning of the Northern Wei Dynasty and continued in the Northern Zhou Dynasty, Sui Dynasty, the Five Dynasties, Song Dynasty and the Xixia Regime in succession. The repair work is never suspended. Among 22 caves, Cave 7, Cave 9and Cave 22 were excavated in the Northern Wei Dynasty; Cave 8, Cave 11, Cave 12, Cave 13and Cave 21 were in the Northern Zhou Dynasty; Cave 4, Cave 10 and Cave 15 were in the Sui Dynasty; Cave 2, Cave 3, Cave 5, Cave 6, Cave 14, Cave 16, Cave 17and Cave 18 were in the Tang Dynasty; Cave 1 and Cave 19 were in the Five Dynasties as well as the Cave 20 was in the Yuan Dynasty. The later dynasties frequently re-built caves upon the former and repaired them.

The buildings, statues and murals comprise the art of Western Thousand Buddha Grotto, the same as that of other Grottoes in Dunhuang region. With regard to the layout and subject of it, they altered along with the aesthetic change of the day. Three different cave shapes can be seen there as follows: Meditation-cave, it has a square-shaped main room where niches and statues on its frontispiece and side small meditation rooms for monks. In Cave 4 of the Sui Dynasty, the contents on its eastern wall can be seen in Cave 5 excavated in the Tang Dynasty. Some meditation rooms only present a form. Cave 1 and Cave 2 were excavated upon monastic rooms. Cave 2 is a memorial to a Huihu Buddhist master. In it, a monk's statue being molded upon his skeleton ever centered on the western wall, regrettably, it's damaged in 1950's only with a picture left just behind it. In picture, two calabashes and a cloth-bag hang on a tree, the man attendant and female attendant stand under it. The second cave shape: Stupa-pillar shaped cave, it prevails in early caves in Western Thousand Buddha Grotto. Rectangle-shaped cave has a square and stupa-shaped pillar centered with a little deviation. The inverted stupa-shaped pillar reaches cave top and being convenient for monks and disciples to worship Buddha images around. The third cave shape: truncated pyramid in shape, it prevails in Western Thousand Buddha Grotto after the Sui and Tang Dynasties. Square-shaped cave with truncated pyramid shape top where beautiful patterns was pained on the square ceiling.

Few statues especially those of the Mid-Tang and Late-Tang Dynasty are in actual existence in Western Thousand Buddha Grotto except for a few early sculptures in several caves there. The statues of the Qing Dynasty and the Republic of

China (1912-1949) are clumsy in design and vulgar in color, saying nothing of their artistic value. The original style of early statues is still existed. The Gandhara art can be seen in Cave 17 excavated in the north Wei Dynasty where the Buddha statue was molded sitting with legs crossed and soles upward; plump figure, high nose, slim eyes, kindly and amiable looks, looking down in calm together characterize Buddha image. Buddha's standing image below the eastern wall in Cave 12 excavated in the northern Wei Dynasty is original well preserved. The bare-footed Buddha stands on lotus throne with bobbed hairs, ample forehead, broad and heavy shoulder, stalwart physique as well as wears kasaya. It seems a massive head to its body, all these characterize the early statues in history.

The statue is the focus of Buddhist cave. The mural can reflect the theme most favorably and be introduced widely because of its flexible technique and rich subject matter. Western Thousand Buddha Grotto and Mogo grotto share the same shape, structure and artistic style except for few differences in others. Western Thousand Buddha Grotto and Mogo grotto share the same shape, structure and artistic style except for few differences in others. The former, backing on and facing mountains, becomes Dunhuang's scenic spot nowadays.

Sinkiang

Sinkiang, situated in the China's northwest frontier, occupies 1.65 million square kilometers, i.e. one-sixth of the national total area, it's the largest one of all provinces and regions in China. Early in the 13th century B.C., the communication between Sinkiang and the inland came into forth. The traffic line was extended to the central Asia, the south Asia and Europe via Sinkiang after Zhang Qian's two missions to the Western Lands. In the later 1500 years, the precious goods of China and foreign countries were traded on it. Of which, Chinese silk was typical which ever being called "Seles" by the west originally. The modern scholars call this traffic line "the Silk-road". The Silk-road of the day, as it was the bond in history, joined the ancient culture along the Yellow River and the Ganges to the Greek and Persia culture. The total length of the Silk-road whose middle section being within Sinkiang is over 7000 km. Most romantic stories related to the Silk-road had ever happened in Sinkiang region where the oriental and Hesperian civilization had blended into each other as well. In the Han Dynasty, the Silk Road within Sinkiang mainly comprised the southern and northern route mainly. The route north of the Mount Tianshan became prosperous latterly and being called the northern route. In the Sui and Tang Dynasties, the southern, middle and northern routes constituted the Silk-road in Sinkiang as follows:

The southern route: referring to the route between the northern foot of Mount Kunlun and the southern verge of Taklimakan Desert. It went westward via Yangguan Pass, the southern verge of Bailongdui Desert, Shanshan state (i.e. original Loulan state, Sinkiang's Ruoqiang county nowadays), Qiemo county, Jingjue state (i.e. the north of Sinkiang's Mingfeng county nowadays), Yutian state (i.e. the north of Sinkiang's Hetian county nowadays), Shache state (i.e. the north of Sinkiang's Shache county nowadays), Chongling (i.e. the Pamirs nowadays), Afghanixtan, Persia (i.e.Iran) or India in turn.

The middle route: referring to the route to Chongling along the southern foot of Mount Tianshan and the northern verge of Taklimakan Desert. It went westward via Yumen Pass (its site being situated in the northwest Dunhuang city nowadays), Gaochang state (i.e. Sinkiang's Turpan nowadays), the southern foot of Mount Tianshan, Weixu state (i.e. Sinkiang's Hesuo county nowadays), the Yanqi state (i.e. Sinkiang's Yanqi county nowadays), Qiuci state (i.e. Sinkiang's Kuche county nowadays), Gume state (i.e. Sinkiang's Akesu city nowadays), Shule state (i.e. Sinkiang's Kashi city nowadays) and Chongling (i.e. the Pamirs nowadays) in turn.

The northern route: referring to the route north of Mount Tianshan. It went to Caspian coastland via Yumen Pass, Yiwu state (i.e. Sinkiang's Hami county nowadays), Pu'nei state (i.e. Sinkiang's Balikan county nowadays), Beiting city (i.e. Sinkiang's Jimsar county nowadays), Gongyue city (i.e. Sinkiang's Huocheng county nowadays) and Yili region in turn.

Sinkiang lies on the middle section of the Silk-road and to be thought of the center where economic and cultural exchanges had been carried out between the east and the west from ancient time. The total length of the Silk-road in Sinkiang was more than thousands of kilometers and most oases and cities there were linked. Countless ruins of ancient cities, cultural relics, scenic sites as well as local conditions and customs left by ancient people along the Silk-road catch tourists' eyes nowadays. They are real portraitures of the ancient brilliant culture in the Western Lands.

All these relics are valuable and reflect the characteristics of Sinkiang's culture of the day. The ancient oases and cities covered by sands for thousands years, enigmatical ancient tombs and mummies, temples and grottoes, the site of Yili Gen. mansion, the latter-day and modern ethical tombs as well as the Islamic worship towers and Mosques can be seen everywhere. The tourists will really understand the glorious history of the day while wandering about along the old Silk-road, reading ancient books preserved in museum, watching jade from Mount Kunlun, listening to the story about Mount Tianshan, seeking for historical relics and judging antiques. Many pendent mysteries under Taklimakan Desert wait for scholars to study and explain.

Tianchi Lake

Tianchi Lake

Tianchi Lake, situated at the mountainside of the Bogeda Peak in Sinkiang's Fukang County nowadays, 110km to Urumqi city in the east, is a natural mountain lake at a height of 1980 m above sea level and being encircled by 18 modern glaciers, 3 rivers and 18 small lakes. Of which, Tianchi Lake is the biggest.

There are 200 species of plant (mainly the pine tree), 20-odd species of animal, over 50 species of bird in Mount TianShan. Tianchi Lake, situated at the eastern section of Mount Tianshan, takes half-moon shape with 3400m in its circumference, 1500m in maximum width, 105m in maximum depth and 4.9 square kilometers in the area. The azure, sparkling and crystal-clear water is surrounded by hills where tier upon tier of pine trees are growing, and blotting out the sky and covering the sun, luxuriant and bluish green and blossoms can be seen everywhere. The summit of the Bogeda Peak at a height of 5,445 m above Sea level stands at the southeast Tianchi Lake and being accompanied by two penholder-shaped peaks on its both sides. The snow-capped main peak and Tianchi Lake set off each other to advantage. The azure water will cool tourists in hot summer. In summer, tourists shall feel chilly while making a boating excursion on Tianchi Lake, they have to wear woolen sweater against cold weather there, it's the fairyland for those who coming from the Gobi desert to spend their summer. They will forget themselves while stepping into Tianchi Lake in summer.

As a legend goes that Tianchi Lake to be the palace of Queen Mother of the West. Queen Mother of the West ever named it Binchi, Longtan, Shenchi and Xianchi. In the Qing Dynasty, MingLiang, a commander-in-chief of one of the Eight Banners (military-administrative organizations of the Man nationality in the Qing Dynasty) who stationed troops at Urumuqi, one day, he led troops to climb Mount Bogeda. He dug a trench to draw Lake water down mountain and in the meanwhile wrote a record of it and had it inscribed on a tablet, i.e. record of digging a trench from Tianchi Lake. Tianchi Lake accordingly came to the top. Many temples had ever been built nearby it, such as Fushou Temple, Queen Mother Temple, Taoist WuJi temple and Immortal Temple, etc. Regrettably, all of them are preserved.

In 1994, the way to Tianchi Lake was opened. Tianchi Lake becomes a famous spot. In 1971,GuoMo-ruo, a celebrated man in China, visited Tianchi Lake and was intoxicated by it. He said in the following poem that Tianchi Lake is azure as it were a inkstone filled with ink, pine trees being reflected in it look like brushes, the artistic conception of it thus can be seen. In 1982, the state the national state council listed Tianchi Lake in the directory for the first group of national key scenic spots. The perfect tourist facilities there make Tianchi Lake the all-important site for the east and west tourists to visit in Sinkiang.

Sugong Minaret

Sugong Minaret, alias Emin Minaret, 44 m high, lies at the spot 2 km to the east Turpan city, was built with yellow bricks in 1779. Many geometrical patterns can be found there. The Minaret's top is covered with green glazed tiles together with "Kubo"(i.e. a Islamic decorative pattern on the iron pole) and crescent sign being at its top erectly. 72-storied spiral staircase can be seen inside the Minaret, the visitors can reach its top along it and overlook the beautiful Turpan oasis.

The magnificent, classical style, grand and impressive structure, lark appearance and cone-shaped outline together characterize Sugong Minaret. It's the highest Islamic tower in China and being accompanied by a Mosque nearby. The Mosque is so spacious that 1000-odd Muslims can make worship within it. The Mosque's arched ceiling and round top show religious atmosphere very much.

In the period of Qianlong's reign in the Qing Dynasty, Turpan's Uygur Headman Eminkhwajah was conferred upon the title of Zhenguogong(i.e. an honourable reputation in the Qing Dynasty) for his merit to help the Qing government suppress Khwajah's rebellion. Sulaiman, Eminkhwajah's second son, built Emin Minaret in memory of his father and to show his loyalty to the Qing Dynasty. Sulaiman expended 7000 liang(a unit of measurement in ancient China)silver on building it and in the meanwhile he erected a stone tablet to record this event, the name of Sugong Minaret just came of it.

The Appearance of the Magnificent.

Ruins of Gaochang City

In the 1st century B.C., the Han's General DunBi was sent to do western expedition by the Emperor Wu. On their way to the western Lands, General DunBi discovered a place with its perfect terrain suitable to build a fort and to station troops there. From that time on, this place became prosperous and the name "Gaochang" just came of it latterly.

The Ruins of Gaochang city is situated at the Huoyanshan village in Sinkiang, 50 km to southeast Tulufan city. It is called "Yiduhu" by Weiwuer nationality, i.e. the "Capital city". The ancient city covers the area of two million square meters with its wall being built with earth tamped, the highest remnant wall is 11.5 m owing to the earth's fine mucosity. As recorded in book that 12 city gates were in ancient Gaochang city together with many buildings in close order there, for example, the workshops, markets, temples and houses. 30000 local dwellers and 3000 monks had ever lived there.

The Ruins of Gaochang City.

The outside city, inner city together with the official residence constituted the Gaochang city of the day with its lay-out being similar to Chang'an city of the day. Many sites of ancient buildings still can be seen everywhere in the Ruins of Gaochang city. That of a temple is in southwest Ruins of Gaochang city with its door, square, hall, niches and pagodas being well preserved. In Spring of the 2nd year of the period of Zhenguan of the Tang Dynasty (i.e.628A.D), the Buddhist master Hsuan-tsang had ever given the sermon at Gaochang city for more than a month while going on a pilgrimage for sutras. The site of his teaching room is still in actual existence nowadays. The ancient 1300 years-old Gaochang city, being built in the 1st century B.C. and being called Gaochangbi initially, was an important city on the Silk Road of the day. The Gaochang Prefecture, Gaochang regime, XiZhou, Gaochang Huihu regime and Hunzhou had ever connected themselves closely with this place. It is regretful for people that the famous Gaochang city was destroyed by the war in the 14th century A.D.

Many sites of buildings are preserved in the Ruins of Gaochang city. A broad and plain way goes from the northern entrance of the city to the temples southeast of the Ruins of Gaochang city. As to the history of it, it's pendent. The foot passengers, carriages as well as the vehicles can run on it nowadays. The remnant buildings at both sides of the path will arouse tourists' curiosities of what had ever happened in this city of the day. The story related to Gaochang King and Hsuan-tsang will emerge from their mind.

In the 2nd year of the period of Zhenyuan of the Emperor TangTai-zhong's reign (i.e.628A.D.), Hsuan-tsang went on a pilgrimage for sutras. Hsuan-tsang crossed the Moheyan Desert where neither bird nor beast could be seen. He came to Yiwu (i. e. Simkiang's Hami nowadays). Hsuan-tsang wanted to go northwest from Yiwu via Kehanfutu town (i.e. the ruins of Beiting in Simkiang's Jimsar County nowadays). Gaochang King QuWen-tai of the day promptly sent a envoy together with tens of steed to Yiwu to receive Hsuan-tsang while hearing about him. Hsuan-tsang failed in refusing Quwentai's great kindness. He had to enter into Gaochang state after a 6 days' walk. Hsuan-tsang was warmly received and a long talk with Quwentai at that very night. Quwentai, together with his princess, ministers and Buddhist masters there, visited Hsuan-tsang frequently and advised him to stay at Gaochang state and carry forward Buddhism there. Quwentai intentionally invited Hsuan-tsang to live the house nearby the King palace and sent soldiers to guard him. Hsuan-tsang refused their suggestion politely.

Hsuan-tsang decided to say good-bye to Quwentai after tens of days' stay in Gaochang. Quwentai insisted on detaining him, he said that he would follow and attend Hsuan-tsang, so did all people in Gaochang state on the condition that Hsuan-tsang cancelled his original plan. Hsuan-tsang gave him affirmative refusal, he said that even his body stayed here and his mind was wandering. Neither of them gave in. Quwentai did his best to attend Hsuan-tsang, he sent three meals by himself to Hsuan-tsang everyday, but Hsuan-tsang refused them to show his attitude. Hsuan-tsang insisted on refusing food for 4days and Quwentai was touched. He asked Hsuan-tsang to become his sworn brother and stay Gaochang for 3 years after coming back from the west, by then, they would attend Hsuan-tsang and listen to him. Before leaving Gaochang state, Hsuan-tsang made another month of sermon there, Quwentai held the censer to welcome Hsuan-tsang, knelt on the ground before 300 disciples every time and asked Hsuan-tsang to go to the rostrum by stepping on his back.

Before Hsuan-tsang's leaving, all monks, ministers and common people of Gaochang city came to see him off, Quwentai personally accompanied him to have a tens of miles' march.

Bezklik Grotto

Bezklik Grotto, one of Gaochang grottoes, is situated on the cliff west of Motou River bank and 30km to the northeast Sinkiang's Tulufan Basin. It backs on the Mount Flame, faces a small valley where a stream gurgling and babbling as well as being surrounded by poplar trees. The quiet surrounding is a good place for cultivating one-self and meditation. Bezklik Grotto was excavated in the times of the Gaochang Qu's reign (i.e. the times of the Southern and Northern Dynasties). The crest of it was in the times of Gaochang Huihu's regime and felling in the times of theYuan Dynasty.

Bezklik Grotto.

83 numbered grottoes are in actual existence nowadays. Of which, 40-odd grottoes have murals within them. As to the shape and structure of them, Caitya -shaped and Piheluo-shaped grottoes take majority. The niche there was excavated in following ways: one was to excavate them on cliff directly; the other was to build them with adobes on a certain platform connected to a cliff. The square or rectangle-shaped interior characterizes them. As to the top shape of them, most grottoes take straight top, some take arch or flat top, the rest take cylinder-shaped top. 1200-oddm^2 murals with their rich contents can be found in Bezklik Grotto. For example the Life-Story of Buddha, Stories of Buddha's Previous incarnations, Story of Predestination; Thousand Buddha's figures and donor's as well as minority donor's around the standing Buddha. The sutra's illustrations such as that of Sukhavativyuha sutra, Lotus sutra, Bhaisajya sutra and Amita sutra, etc are seen there. The Life-Story of Buddha is painted horizontally in the form of picture-story. The main contents of the sutra's illustrations are centered with those relevant images being painted on its both sides and lower part. Many inscriptions written by donors in both Chinese and Huihu languages are still can be seen. They are the rare materials for studying the grotto history. The Bezklik Grotto was ever a royal temple of the Huihu King of Gaochang state of the day. The Huihu King's portrait could be seen in Cave 45 excavated in the Song Dynasty. As stated in Huihu inscription that Huihu King, wearing peach-shaped crown and being as brave as a lion and an eagle, dominated Gaochang state. The figures of 18 donors in their finery and holding flowers are painted together with their Huihu inscriptions on a wall in Cave 20. It's the only existing mural of a group of donors in Gaochang region.

Scene of Buddha with worshipers Late Tang(618-907,A. D).Wall painting of the grotto No. 20. One of several big paintings showing jataka story, whose greater part had been taken off by Germen in the beginning of this centruy. In the middle stands the Buddha with some worshipers, camel, and horse, etc around him. A kind of colour, reddish brown which the Uighurians liked, was used to paint this picture.

Bezklik Grotto, Cave 69.

The royalty and noble of the Huihu's regime excavated and managed Bezklik Grotto. It is the only grotto to completely represent Huihu's Buddhist art of the day throughout the country. It's the important historical materials to study Huihu people's belief and its development. The relevant illustrations and images of Huihu's sutras and donors can be found in Mogao Grotto, Yulin Grotto and Kezier Grotto being adjacent to Bezklik Grotto. Regrettably, they are inferior to those in Bezklik Grotto whose scale, area of murals and quantity of statues being interior to those of other grottoes.

The Chinese and ancient Huihu, Boluomi as well as Tuhuoluo character and Sanscrit, etc can be found in the inscriptions there which are valuable historical materials to study the culture, history and the language in the Western Lands. From the end of the 19th century to the early stages of the 20th century, foreign adventurer, such as Locker from Germany, Stein from Britain and others from Russia, Japan, etc. looted a lot of murals, statues and ancient books from Bezklik Grotto. They did great damage to the murals by taking it off the wall. In 1982, Bezklik Grotto was listed in the directory of national key cultural relics.

Bezklik Grotto, Cave 69.

Bodhisattvas, komtura Grotto, The Dynasy(618-907)

Komtura Grotto and its Murals

Komtura Grotto, one of famous grottoes on the Silk-road, is situated at the eastern bank of Weigan River 30km to the southwest Sinkiang's Kuche County nowdays. 112 grottoes in total in Komtura Grotto excavated in the 4th century are assigned a number respectively. Its murals are essential part of Qiuci mural art. As to the contents and form of it are similar to those of Kezier Grotto but greatly changed after the Tang's Anxi Douhu office being moved into Qinci in the 7th century. The huge illustrations of Pure Land Sutra, Oriental Bhaisajyagura Sutra, Sukhavativyuha Sutra, etc. as well as sceneries of the mountain, river and building could be seen there owing to the influence of the Buddhist art in central plains. The contents of murals and their line in drawing were close to those of the central plains'. The Huihu people had moved westward and built a Kingdom since the middle stages of the 9th century. It resulted in the appearance of murals being influenced by Huihu art style. Its contents included Buddha's figures, Buddha's Life-story, the predestination of the Buddha's figure and its donor and the illustration of Buddha's Doings based upon a huge centered Buddha's standing figure. The drawing line that combined the painting style of Qiuci with that of the central plains is effective and vivid. The plump and high-colored figures together with the horizontal inscribed boards written in both Chinese and Huihu language can be seen there. It's very close to that in Becklik Grotto, Komtura Grotto accordingly is thought of the history relic of ancient Qiuci as well as the relative of Bezklik Grotto.

Loulan

Loulan, one of 36 states in the Western Lands in the Western Han Dynasty, as recorded in Records of Historian that it chose Gushi as the capital. In 77B.C., King ChangGui acted in collusion with the Hun to hinder the envoy of the Eastern Han Dynasty from entering into to the Western Lands. The Han's General HuoGuang angered it and sent Minister Pingyuejian (an official title in ancient Chine) FuJie-zi to putout him. WeiTu-qi, the younger brother of King ChangGui and ever being sent to serve the Han's emperor in Chang'an, was ordered to return to Loulan state in company with official seal, lady-in-waiting and troops granted imperially to accede to the throne upon King ChangGui's death and Loulan state was renamed as ShanShan state with its capital being moved south to Han'ni town. The former capital (i.e. Gushi) became into the Han's important place to station troops and to open up wasteland and grow food grain. The Loulan lost trace in history from this time on. In the times of the Three Kingdoms and the Western Jin Dynasty, Xuyi Xiaowei (an official title in ancient China) stationed Gaochang and The Western Lands's Adjutant were set. In the early stages of the 20th century, many ancient wooden slips, relics of documents had been unearthed in Loulan city ruins. The textual research showed that the Western Lands's Adjutant had ever stationed at Loulan city within later Shanshan state. Loulan city became derelict drastically by the end of the Former Liang in the 4th century.

Ancient Loulan city located at the spot west of Luobu Lake and 7km to the southern bank of Kongque River, 200km to the northeast Ruoqiang County in Sinkaing nowadays. The existing ancient Loulan city ruins only refer to it in the 4th century. The square outline with magnificent Buddhist pagodas and temples was situated in the northeast Loulan city of the day. In the Han Dynasty, Loulan state was the place with lakes and marshes, being beautiful and rich upon Loubu lake although being a state inside the Asia. It's the key position of the Silk-road of the day and a strategic and large city where both east and west culture blended into each other. Loulan state had its own language and character, many people such as the Hans and Hunnish, Rouzhi, Wuxun, Dawan as well as Sute people ever visited Loulan state successively. As to the question that which race Loulan people pertained to is pendent. Around the time of the 4th century, the Loulan state withered away and its people migrated to other areas and the city ruins came out. The original beautiful Loubu Lake can never be seen together with the prosperity in former days. In the history, the bell on camel's neck was ringing all day long in Loulan city which had been the trade center and transfer station for goods from central plains, Persia, India, Syria and Rome as well as the Hot Spot attracted the eyes of the Hans, Huns and other nomads around.

In 73A.D., BanChao led 36 heroic men to make a mission to the Western Lands and being warmly entertained by Shangshang King. A few days late, Hunnish delegation also came to Shangshang state. BanChao, being a hero who gave up civilian pursuits to join the army, he called his 36 retinues together in time and told them all they were in dangerous situation now, "The only way to catch tiger cubs is to go into tiger's den! ". What they could do was to kill Hun's envoy by a surprise action so that the Shan Shan state could be stabilized and disengaged from Hun state. At nightfall, he in conjunction with his 36 heroic men struck drums, set fire to Hun's tents, rushed into Hun's envoy tent and killed him, after that he invited the king of Shan Shan state and told him what had happened, and the advantages and disadvantages of it. Finally, the king of Shan Shan state decided to break off the relation with Hun state. In the 5th century, Buddhist master FaXian of the Eastern Jin Dynasty passed by here while going on a pilgrimage for sutras. He recorded it in his book that neither bird nor beast could be seen everywhere except for sands blown by terrible hot wind, skeletons there were only road-signs to guide the way. By the time of the Tang Dynasty, Loulan frequently appeared in poems related to the border areas. Li Bai known as a poet in Tang Dynasty ever said in his poem: "wishing to kill the enemy in Loulan with my sword! ". It's the memory related to what had happed in ancient Loulan state.

It is a pendent that what had happened in Loulan city, a well-known city in the Han Dynasty. Did there happen a war, the quicksand or other? When did the Loulan city be abandoned? Where did the people there go? No one can answer it nowadays with exception of the unearthed wooden slips and fragments of pottery and silk and fabrics as well as the silent Buddha towers.

Ancient Luolan city ruins.

The Lop Nur Ancient Corpse Unearthed at Ancient Tomb Valley.

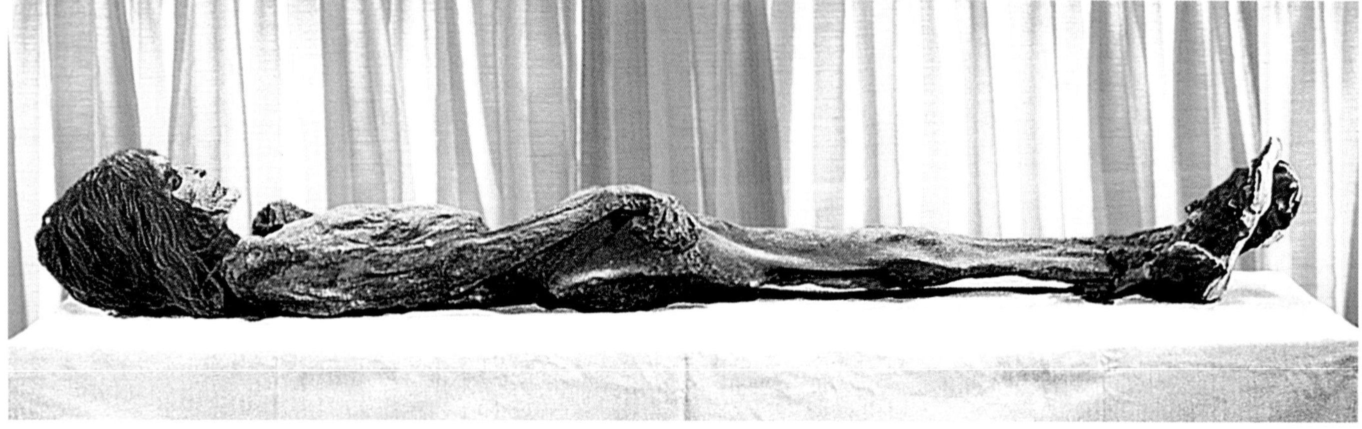

Loulan's Beauty

In 1980, at Sinkiang's Tieban River delta (i.e. site of ancient Loulans state) in China, an earliest and well-preserved ancient lady corpse being named Loulan's Beauty was unearthed by Archeological Institute in Sinkiang Social Science Academy. Both the international archaeological and medical world concern themselves about it as soon as it being unearthed because of its unparalleled archaeological and medical value. The scientists from Sinkiang archeological and medical worlds, Shanghai's Medical College, Natural Museum and Biochemistry Institution of ASC has researched it for 10-odd years. The research result showed that the 3800 years-old Loulan's Beauty died at his age of 40. She is 152 cm in her stature (155.8cm before her death) and 10.7kg in weight; O-type blood and European race.

After having dissected the corpse of ancient lady, the medical expert found that internal organs of the corpse were preserved entirely, that internal organs including heart, lung, liver, stomach, kidney, spleen, bladder, large intestine, small intestine, uterus or so, these internal organs changed into stiffening and diminishing, the hairs of corpse were elastic, the medical expert could make out the shape of lung of corpse, there were black dusts in the lung of corpse of ancient lady, which showed that lived in the desert area while she was living.

The medical experts anatomized Loulan's Beauty and found that her shrink and dried innards such as heart, liver, lung, kidney, spleen, cyst, large and small intestine as well as uterus are still well preserved, the flexibility of her hairs cab be felt and her lung shape can be identified. The many black atomies there showed that she had ever lived in a desert with sands blown by violent wind before her death.

The dry climate and hot weather together with the gale and sandstorm there quickly made her corpse lose water and delayed oxidization before decaying. The Loulan's Beauty's tomb was built in a high platform 7¡«8 m above the ground and far away from being submerged by water. One meter deep grave where the corpse was covered with well ventilated and evaporated sands, reed poles and Chinese tamarisk branches. The Loulan's Beauty was dead in winter, the freezing weather restrained movement of bacteria.

TianLin, a Sinkiang cultural relic expert, discovered a kind of coating on the Loulan's Beauty's corpse unexpectedly while treating it for protection. The popular conclusion that ancient mummy being air-dried by nature confronts with oppugner accordingly.

The 3800 years-old Loulan's Beauty is a rare mummy and a specimen for parasitology in the world. The protein coating on the 3800year-old mummy is too thin to discover. TianLin testified that the coating on mummies unearthed at Zhahongluke's in Sinkiang's Qiemo County was also found while she was treating it. These tumuli were built in 10th century B.C., where TianLin discovered the lark coating 0.1¡« 0.5mm thick on an adult, old and infantile mummies.

The sample analysis negated the possibility that the coating being mineral or starchiness except for being a kind of unknown protein owing to being enslaved to the outlay and techniques. But it's affirmative that the existence of coating keeps the mummy from decay during 3800 years.

Worship in Mosque

Mosque

Mosque, alias the bethel, is called "Maisi Jide" (i.e. building where Muslims worship Allah) and "Baitunla" as well (i.e. the Allah's residence) in Arabic as well as Qingtingsi, Qingxiusi, Jingjuesi, Famingsi, Zhenjiaosi and Islamic bethel, etc. in Chinese history. Mosque has become the exclusive name of Chinese Islamic bethel since the middle part of the Ming Dynasty. The Islamic scholar annotates Mosque (i.e. Qingzhensi in Chinese) in philosophical words as follows: "Qing" represents Allah being preeminent and immanent and "Zhen" represents Allah being immortal and unique. Muslims accordingly consider Mosque the lustration and saintly place. The practical but beautiful in its appearance and elegant in its structure just characterize it.

Mosque is generally centered at an area of dense Muslims. To live around Mosque constitutes one of characteristics of Chinese Muslim. The worship hall, teaching room, worship tower, the classroom, and baptistery together make up of Mosque. The worship hall in Mosque where Muslims worshiping Allah is built towards east. The teaching room where the mullah teaching imam the Koran is set in front of the worship hall.

Early Mosque in China took Arab architectural style in its shape. The earliest Muslims came from west by ship during the Tang and Song Dynasties. Mosque of the day was built at ports along coast of southeast China. The architectural style of Mosque greatly used traditional Chinese buildings for reference since the Song and Yuan Dynasties. The Chinese buildings assimilate the Mosque's architectural style from the west. More and more Muslim's communities and Mosques appeared in northwest China along the Silk-road of the day. They basically took the shape of the traditional Chinese square courtyard. The colorful decoration marks the Chinese Mosque outstandingly and exclusively. Most Mosques have blended the Islamic decoration style with those of Chinese traditional building. They give priority to the harmony of the architectural complex's color. Many decoration style such as the flower pattern, geometrical pattern together with Arab words are take in Mosque shape, it makes the Islamic substances stand out.

Most newly-built Mosques in the northwest China gave much attention to the whole colorway while decorating them in part or wholly. They were decorated with gypseous floriation, paintings, brick carvings and woodcarvings or so being changeable in kind, color, craftwork as well as style and patterns. The Chinese Mosque's style thus can be seen. Hezhou brick carving is known as the fine art-ware. In short, as to the space arrangement, outline, painting and carving, the diversity gives much to the newly-built mosques in northwest China every-way. It shows that endless vitality and creativity exist in the Chinese Mosque.

Postscript

Silk-road, a thoroughfare from the ancient central plains stretched towards the west upon the Chinese ancient silk trade. Both the southern and northern routes of it started from Chang'an (i.e.Xi'an city nowadays) respectively and finally arrived in Dunhuang via Hexi Corridor. Of witch, one route was out of the Yumen Pass, then reached Rome Empire of the day via Qianwangting of Chesshi state, Qiuci state, Shule state, Congling (i.e. Pamir nowadays), Middle Asia and West Asia in turn; the another route was out Yangguan Pass and finally arrived in Rome Empire of the day via LouLan state, Yutian state, Congling (i.e.Pamir nowadays), Darouzhi and Anxi states in turn, total 7 000-odd km in whole length. In the 2nd century B. C., the Emperor Wu of the Han Dynasty twice sent Zhang Qian on a diplomatic mission to the Western Lands, the road to the west was opened thereout which brought convenience to the communication between ancient China and the Middle Asia than previous times. Large quantities of Chinese silks were transported to the west along this road, "Silk-road" just came of it. The opening of it not only joined the inland with Mount Tianshan areas but also established a close relationship in economy and culture between the ancient central plains and the West Lands or even far regions. The Chinese other materials besides the silk, for example, the metallic tools, cast irons and paper-making technologies were introduced to the Europe via the Middle Asia; In the meanwhile, products from the Middle Asia, West Asia, South Asia and Europe were carried to the central plains in succession and in force via Hexi region. They benefited people's lives in both Hexi region and central plains, some of them were agricultural seeds, such as those of grape, clover blossom, til, safflower, coriander, onion, garlic, broad bean, cucumber, rare birds and animals as well as woolies and fine breed horses and camel. The Buddhism and its art were introduced to the West Lands via the Middle Asia as well, then to the east. History has left the Silk-road with large quantities of cultural relics, such as the ruins of ancient cities, tombs, the Great Wall, religion temples and grottoes. The tens of thousands of cultural relics unearthed at Dunhuang grottoes and the ancient tombs in Sinkang's Turpan relate to the history and culture of ancient countries and nationalities in China, Middle Asia, South Asia and West Asia. The Silk-road greatly played important role in the economic and cultural exchanges between ancient China and the West. To lucubrate the 2000-odd years of history of Silk-road becomes the scholars' aim nowdays.

Silk-road, as it were an old song or a romantic verse, is eternal. It, for its charms, attracts numerous tourists to recall ancient Chinese splendor and create their beautiful futures along with the constant development of northwest China, greater and greater prosperous in Chinese economy, culture and increasing individual income as well as more and more people paying attention to tour out. We have a long-cherished wish to write a book about the Silk-road. Many various subjects are involved in the brilliant history of the Silk-road, therefore, we only have generally introduced famous cultural relics on Silk-road and Dunhuang, the distribution station on the Silk-road of the day, in this book because that Dunhuang's history and art to be thought of the representative of that of the Silk-road. No books can fully describe and include its cultural values and artistic contents. This book, for its knowledge and interest, is of much great benefit to readers to understand both Silk-road and Dunhuang art. We have used the study results of other writers (seeing references for details) for reference while writing this book. Thanks to these writers and Ms. Fan Jinshi, the Director of Dunhuang Academy, for their great help.

Reference

Silk Road Periodical , Silk Road Editor Board(1995～2001 bound edition)
Silk Road Dictionary, Hongqi Press (Aug., 1995)
Dunhuang Study Dictionary, Shanghai Dictionary Press (Dec., 1998)
Gansu Ancient History, Gansu People's Press (Oct., 1991)
Jiuquan, Gansu Educational Press (July, 1996)
Silk Road Visit, Gansu People's Press (Apr., 1983)
Silk Road Documents Record, Lanzhou Press (Sep., 1989)
Silk Road, Gansu People's Press (Mar., 1988)
Silk Road's History, Gansu People's Press (July, 1983)
Ancient Travellers on Silk Road, Sinkang Youth Press (Dec., 1993)
Pilgrimagers For Sutras Along Silk Road, Gansu People's Press (May, 1991)
Dunhuang's History and Culture, Xinhua Press (Dec., 1993)
Gansu's Silk Road History, Gansu People's Press (Mar., 1986)
Gansu's Tourism Culture, Lanzhou University Press (May, 1994)
Wester Lands Treasures, Sinkang People's Press (Sep., 1999)
Silk Road Guide- Sinkang, Sinkang Art & Photography Press (May, 1994)
Tourism on Silk Road, Guangdun Tourist Press (May, 1999)
Silk Road Guide- Gansu, Gansu People's Press (Aug., 1992)
Famen Temple, Sanqin Press (Apr., 1988)
Silk Road Guide, Shanxi Press Tourist Press (Feb., 1987)
Dunhuang's History, Changjiang Literature &Art Press (Mar., 2002)
Mogao Grotto, Knowledge Press (Oct., 1995)
Dunhang's Story Murals, Gansu People's Press (Dec., 1991)
Sutra's Story, Chinese Literature and History Press (Nov., 1996)
Sakyamuni's Biography, Jilin People's Press (May, 1993)
Dunhuang's Culture, Guangming Daily Press (Dec., 2000)
Buddhist History in Western Lands, Sinkang Art & Photography Press (Oct., 1998)
Chinese Grottoes-Dunhuang Mogao-Grotto(Vol.1～5), Cultural Relic Press(Mar., 1987)
Chinese Grotto Collection- Sinkang Turpan, Liaoning People's Art Press (Mar., 1990)
Chinese Grottoes-Anxi Yulin Grotto, Cultural Relic Press (May., 1997)
Dunhuang's Grotto, Gansu Culture Press (May, 1998)
Dunhuang, Zhaohua Press (Jan.2000)
Dunhuang Flying Devi, Chinese Tourist Press (Oct., 1993)
Dunhuang in China, Jiangsu Art Press (Jun., 2000)
Dunhuang, Jiangsu Art Press (July, 1990)
Gansu, Gansu People's Press (Sep., 1984)
Dunhuang, Chinese Environmental Science Press (Mar., 1997)
To Sinkang, Sinkang Art Press (Jun., 1998)
Dunhuang Flying Devi, Gansu People's Press (Sep., 1995)